The Secret Garden

Marie-Louise von Franz, Honorary Patron

**Studies in Jungian Psychology
by Jungian Analysts**

Daryl Sharp, General Editor

THE SECRET GARDEN

Temenos for Individuation

*A Jungian appreciation of themes
in the novel by Frances Hodgson Burnett*

Margaret Eileen Meredith

To my husband, Schuyler Brown, for his unfailing encouragement

National Library of Canada Cataloguing in Publication Data

Meredith, Margaret Eileen
    The secret garden: temenos for individuation / Margaret
    Eileen Meredith.

(Studies in Jungian psychology by Jungian analysts; 111)
 Includes bibliographical references and index.

ISBN 1-894574-12-5

1. Individuation (Psychology) in literature.
2. Individuation (Psychology).
3. Burnett, Frances Hodgson, 1849-1924, Secret Garden.
I. Title. II. Series.

BF175.5.I53M47 2004   155.2'5   C2004-900779-3

INNER CITY BOOKS
Box 1271, Station Q, Toronto, ON M4T 2P4, Canada

Telephone (416) 927-0355 / FAX (416) 924-1814

Web site: www.innercitybooks.net / E-mail: admin@innercitybooks.net

Honorary Patron: Marie-Louise von Franz.
Publisher and General Editor: Daryl Sharp.
Senior Editor: Victoria Cowan.

INNER CITY BOOKS was founded in 1980 to promote the
understanding and practical application of the work of C.G. Jung.

Cover: Botanical Gardens, Niagara Falls, Canada (photo by the author).

Printed and bound in Canada by University of Toronto Press Incorporated

CONTENTS

See final page for descriptions of other Inner City Books

Preface

The Secret Garden, written by Frances Hodgson Burnett, was first published in 1911. For many, the reading of this story was a pivotal experience of childhood, leaving a mark that is more than memory. It is a realm of reality alive in the imagination, a rosebud in a distant corner of the soul. Over the years of grappling with the tasks of maturation, this rosebud recedes into the distance to become almost imperceptible.

And yet! See the animation, almost reverence, that comes over a person when memories of *The Secret Garden* are evoked. My own response to that book, and in general to the symbolism of secrets and gardens, is tinged with rapture.

The archetypal realm at the heart of any symbol creates an irresistible fascination, which inevitably has a spiritual quality. Thus was I drawn to explore my attraction to *The Secret Garden* and the psychological implications of its many motifs.

Margaret Eileen Meredith

WHO LOVES A GARDEN

STILL HIS EDEN KEEPS.

Figure 1. Original woodcut by Mary Azarian, Vermont.

1
Introduction

The Reality of the Psyche

During my years of exploring the psyche, in my own analytical process as well as with analysands, I have been struck by the paradoxical nature of the endeavor. The paradox lies in the use of language and theory to describe often elusive, ultimately mysterious realms. The effort to become conscious of aspects of one's inner processes requires an appreciation of the psyche, not just a facility with intellectual concepts. This is difficult. Western culture values understanding by way of the intellect. But this is only one of many rich modalities of the psyche.

Jung once remarked that he was unable to communicate the complexity of the psyche to others. He said,

> I am practically alone. There are a few who understand this and that, but almost nobody sees the whole. . . . I have failed in my foremost task: to open people's eyes to the fact that man has a soul and there is a buried treasure in the field.[1]

This passage was discussed in an interview with Edward F. Edinger in 1999. Asked by fellow analyst Lawrence Jaffe whether he thought Jung was better understood now, Edinger replied, "No. Less so, because there are fewer people now—visible to me, anyway—who understand even his basics. It's a very sad sight to see."[2] Later he was asked whether he knew any way to help people stay with the reality of the psyche, a phrase which expresses the essence of Jung's understanding. Edinger replied,

> That's really the big problem because the whole question is *seeing* it. That's all that's required: you just have to *see* it. And apparently all of us

---

[1] Quoted by Gerhard Adler in "Aspects of Jung's Personality," in *Psychological Perspectives*, Spring 1975, p. 14.
[2] "Interview with Edward F. Edinger," in *Journal of Jungian Theory and Practice*, Fall 1999, p. 51.

live on the level of concepts and hence what we talk about are intellectual concepts. . . .

. . . The question of recognizing the reality of the psyche is the whole point of Jungian psychology. That's why Jung says . . . his major task was to open people's eyes to the fact that *man has a soul.* The psyche is real.[3]

However, the psyche and matters psychological are often devalued. Jung noted that phenomena were often dismissed if they were considered to be psychological. This is tantamount to rejecting the inner world of the soul. He expresses his understanding in the following passage:

Psychology is spoken of as if it were "only" psychology and nothing else. The notion that there can be psychic factors which correspond to divine figures is regarded as a devaluation of the latter. It smacks of blasphemy to think that a religious experience is a psychic process; for, so it is argued, a religious experience "is not *only* psychological."[4]

He goes on to reflect upon the implications of such an attitude:

Faced with this situation, we must really ask: How do we know so much about the psyche that we can say "only" psychic? For this is how Western man, whose soul is evidently "of little worth," speaks and thinks. If much were in his soul he would speak of it with reverence.[5]

It is as if the reality of the psyche had been sealed behind a door and the key buried.

Thus my exploration of *The Secret Garden* is undertaken with mindfulness for the delicacy and complexity of the subject, which is not only the beloved story but also the reality and vitality of the psyche.

In *Text and Psyche,* Schuyler Brown explores how the reality of the psyche affects the reading experience. He gives a succinct conceptual description of the intermingling of these phenomena:

The world of the text and the world of psyche are two paths which are destined to intersect, as the key is made for the lock; the energy transfer

---

[3] Ibid., pp. 57f.

[4] *Psychology and Alchemy,* CW 12, par. 9. (CW refers throughout to *The Collected Works of C.G. Jung)*

[5] Ibid., par. 10.

between the two worlds comes about, in Jung's theory, through the agency of the archetypes [primordial, structural elements of the human psyche]. The archetypal imagery of the text corresponds to the archetypal basis of the complexes of the reader.[6] But it is only because the archetype includes both the image and the instinctual emotion that it is able to effect the energy transfer to the psyche of the reader.[7]

I think the key to this venture is to be found in the symbol. It has the potential to lead one to an experience, often ineffable, of ultimate value, bringing with it a certain unique knowledge that points to a region of the mind and soul beyond the reach of language. This way of knowing has been called *apophatic,* a term used to refer to how one contemplates the unknowability of God. Writers in this tradition speak of the value this process has for the fullness of life. It has been summarized as follows:

> There exists within the vast terrain of the human consciousness a dimension that is potentially accessible to anyone drawn to its exploration. It is a dimension in which a unique mode of awareness can occur which the mind, on its return to the familiar concerns of daily existence, will value above all actual or conceivable experiences. An essential requirement for the approach to this dimension is that the mind presses beyond all thought and language, all the familiar naming and conceptual devices used in coping with our complex environment, and confronts the stark, inescapable and irreducible fact of IS.[8]

This IS constitutes the place of being, of nature, where things are as they are, the living tissue of existence.

Robert Browning speaks of the three souls of the human being. The first soul is a doer, with its feet on the ground; the second soul, resting upon the first, knows; the third soul, standing upon the other two, reaches

---

[6] "Complexes are 'feeling-toned ideas' that over the years accumulate around certain archetypes, for instance 'mother' and 'father.' When complexes are constellated, they are invariably accompanied by affect. They are always relatively autonomous." (Daryl Sharp, *Jung Lexicon: A Primer of Terms and Concepts,* p. 38)

[7] *Text and Psyche: Experiencing Scripture Today,* pp. 93f.

[8] Hastings Moore and Gary W. Moore, eds., *The Neighborhood of IS: Approaches to the Inner Solitude,* p. 6.

to the stars. "What Does, What Knows, What Is; three souls, one man."[9]

Symbols and symbolic truth have their roots in the depths of the psyche as well as in the unknown mystery to which the soul responds. Empirical truth is dependent upon the intellect, but symbols are compelling in a manner that facts are not. They have the capacity to free the imagination along with psychic energy. D.H. Lawrence conveys their complex vitality:

> Symbols are organic units of unconsciousness with a life of their own, and you can never explain them away, because their value is dynamic, emotional, belonging to the sense-consciousness of the body and soul, and not simply mental.[10]

He recognizes that this dynamic, emotional characteristic, which is central to their nature, is beyond comprehension:

> A complex of emotional experience is a symbol. And the power of the symbol is to arouse the deep emotional self, and the dynamic self, beyond comprehension. Many ages of accumulated experience still throb within a symbol. And we throb in response.[11]

Symbols and Symbolism

This book is an exploration of the symbol of the secret garden as it relates to and reveals the individuation process, particularly in Jungian analysis. Although each individual's experience in analysis is unique, this symbol does give some intimation of what happens. In general, I hope to convey the quickening of the spirit that gives momentum to the analytic journey. An appreciation of the symbolic world is crucial for this endeavor.

A symbol has the capacity to bring new realizations to consciousness, rather like being struck by an arrow from Eros. There is an impact, an harmonic tone, that brings more openness to life because inner realms resonate in response. When the spirit quickens, the soul also awakens.

---

[9] "A Death in the Desert," in *The Poetical Works of Robert Browning,* p. 386.

[10] *Apocalypse,* p. 48.

[11] Ibid., p. 49.

Figure 2. Eros strings his bow.
(Roman copy of a statue of about 330 B.C.,
by Greek sculptor Lysippus; Rome, Capitoline Museum)

This gives a feeling of the fullness of life in the moment which is also experienced in the body. One senses that yes! This is IT! This is the unalloyed truth! Although, as Jung points out, the psyche itself "remains an insoluble puzzle and an incomprehensible wonder, an object of abiding perplexity,"[12] nevertheless, through the vehicle of the symbol the psyche reveals itself to each of us so that we can partake of the mystery and derive nourishment for the enrichment of our lives.

Jung helps us open to the gift of the living symbol. He says that a symbol is the best possible embodiment of some unknown aspect of the psyche which is full of meaning.[13] He also speaks about how deep calls unto deep: the symbol comes from the depths of the psyche, expressing a living truth that has transformative capability. But, he notes, these processes "should never be given hard and fast names if their living movement is not to petrify into something static."[14] Not only is the symbol a picture of a psychic process,

> it also brings a re-experiencing of it, of that twilight which we can learn to understand only through inoffensive empathy, but which too much clarity only dispels.[15]

The transformative capacity of the symbol resides in its attraction for both consciousness and the unconscious.

> The unconscious can be reached and expressed only by symbols, and for this reason the process of individuation can never do without the symbol. The symbol is the primitive exponent of the unconscious, but at the same time an idea that corresponds to the highest intuitions of the conscious mind.[16]

In short, the symbol is the bridge over which energy and awareness travel within the psyche. The archetypal world at the heart of the symbol exerts an irresistible appeal to the imagination if one is open.

---

[12] *The Undiscovered Self,* p. 56.

[13] "Definitions," *Psychological Types,* CW 6, pars. 814f.

[14] "Paracelsus as a Spiritual Phenomenon," *Alchemical Studies,* CW 13, par. 199.

[15] Ibid.

[16] "Commentary on 'The Secret of the Golden Flower,' " ibid., par. 44.

In spite of the affinity between the psyche and symbols, Jung points out that a great deal depends upon the attitude a person has toward the symbolic world:

> A symbol really lives only when it is the best and highest expression for something divined but not yet known to the observer. It then compels his unconscious participation and has a life-giving and life-enhancing effect.[17]

It is not automatic. The symbol may call. But the individual ego can ignore, reject or disparage the call—to its own impoverishment. However when a symbol is alive for a person it emanates a numinosity which is hard to ignore. It attracts one's attention because it generates an energy approaching desire, even longing, in the person for whom it manifests.

The Numinosity of Symbols

The term "numinous" refers to the experience of the holy without any moral or rational component. It is a compelling feeling which has value and requires attention for its own sake.[18] This is generally associated with experiences related to the Self.

The term "Self" in analytical psychology refers to the totality of the psyche, which includes consciousness and the unconscious, as well as the phenomenon underlying the individuation process specific to each person. The Self is the archetype of wholeness and the regulating center of the psyche, a transpersonal power that transcends the ego. Like any archetype, the essential nature of the Self is unknowable, but it manifests in dreams, myth, legend, fairy tales, art and music:

> In the course of the process of maturation, . . . the various aspects of totality enter the field of consciousness, thus leading to a widening of the continually changing horizon of awareness. Beyond this there is often *a numinous experience of inner psychic wholeness.*[19]

My personal feeling about Hodgson's novel *The Secret Garden* is a special, quiet excitement, a sense of wonder and delight. Indeed, it seems

---

[17] "Definitions," *Psychological Types*, CW 6, par. 819.

[18] See Rudolf Otto, *The Idea of the Holy*, p. 6.

[19] Emma Jung and Marie-Louise von Franz, *The Grail Legend*, p. 98.

that for those of us who love this story, the secret garden, both as story and as metaphor, is preserved intact by the Self, away from the specific interests of the everyday world.

A secret garden bestows radiance into the life of the one who loves it. The soul can hear the spirit whisper in this safe place. It is a container for reflection upon the mysteries of the processes of life and for activity to support them. The ineffable world underlying the physical can be seen within the solitude and stillness of its precinct. Through this tiny window of the secret garden the universe can reveal itself. To witness the matrix of life in which we are embedded can be felt as a revelation.

Joseph Campbell describes such an experience which he had after seeing a scientific movie about protoplasm: it was in constant flux, flowing, shaping everything. After the movie he had an epiphany as he drove down the California coast to Big Sur. He says,

> All I could see was protoplasm in the form of grass being eaten by cows; protoplasm in the form of birds diving for protoplasm in the form of fish. You just get this wonderful sense of the abyss from which all has come. But each form has its own intentions, its own possibilities, and that's where meaning comes. Not in the protoplasm itself.[20]

In the secret garden one can witness the miracles of life and also find meaning.

Story, Imagination and Play

Of course, the secret garden is not only a specific entity such as a story or actual garden. It can also live as a cherished memory or creation, a hot ember glowing in the deep places of the imagination. Thus one of the functions of the secret garden on a symbolic level is to provide an inner place where the imagination can come to life unencumbered.

The gift of imagination is particularly bountiful in childhood:

> It is as if the spiritual birth cord were not cut as soon as the body's, and there were still a great drawing on The Giver of All Things for spiritual sustenance and growth.

---

[20] *The Power of Myth*, p. 211.

But midway in childhood something begins to happen. The cord is cut. There must be adjustment to a factual, material world.[21]

If the connection is not reestablished as the years pass, consciousness becomes too narrow, lacking the revivifying animation that the freedom of the imagination brings. A whole new world of possibilities opens when the imagination is activated, because the habitual activity of the ego is made relative.

A story activates the imagination. It is not only a vehicle for entertainment but also for experience and therefore learning. Often when we reflect on life it is apparent that the most profound learning comes through experience. The imagination is fed by both symbol and story. James Hillman observes:

> As depth psychologist I see that those who have a connection with story are in a better shape and have a better prognosis than those to whom story must be introduced.[22]

We live in a society that emphasizes logic, literalism and materialism. In contrast, stories offer another perspective. "Soul-making," writes Hillman, "goes hand in hand with deliteralizing consciousness and restoring its connection to mythic and metaphorical thought patterns."[23]

When a story is entered, all the psychic faculties—intuition, feeling, sensing and thinking—are activated along with the imagination. This enables a person to participate with freedom in the world of possibilities, as well as with one's ancestral and cultural roots. Since it is life enhancing, this experience is important for the well-being of the psyche. Jung:

> The creative activity of imagination frees man from his bondage to the "nothing but" and raises him to the status of one who plays. As Schiller says, man is completely human only when he is at play.[24]

Let us pause here for a moment to consider play. It is an important psychological element in *The Secret Garden*. Play is older than culture,

---

[21] Ruth Sawyer, *The Way of the Storyteller,* p. 117.

[22] *Loose Ends,* p. 1.

[23] Ibid., p. 3.

[24] "The Aims of Psychotherapy," *The Practice of Psychotherapy,* CW 16, par. 98.

an activity fundamental to life. Yet in adulthood it may seem superfluous since it is not a physical or moral necessity.[25]

Although it does not lend itself to precise definition, play does have three main characteristics. The first is that it is voluntary; it is a free act. Secondly, it occurs outside the necessary activities of daily life but adorns them. Thirdly, it is limited, sometimes secluded in a ritual space. Play "loves to surround itself with an air of secrecy. Even in early childhood the charm of play is enhanced by making a 'secret' out of it."[26]

In the secret garden of the imagination the various functions of consciousness are free to play. The ego, unloosed from its habitual patterns, is more fluid in the present moment. Marie-Louise von Franz believes that when the imagination is activated, the functions of thinking, feeling, sensing and intuiting

> become mere instruments of a consciousness which is no longer rooted in them or in a driven way active within the functions, but has its basis of operation in another dimension, a dimension which can only be created by the world of imagination.[27]

She considers this to be possible because there is a quiet stillness in the inner center.

Jung calls this capacity of the psyche the transcendent function, and says that the creative imagination is "the only primordial phenomenon accessible to us, the real Ground of the psyche, the only immediate reality."[28] Von Franz adds: "It is the divine principle itself."[29]

Imagination gives life color, depth, vitality and intensity. By developing a loving relationship with the creative imagination, the severity engendered by unmitigated, goal-directed activities is softened. Other dimensions of life can penetrate. When the heart can play with the imagination, then the capacity for spontaneity can join with the drive for achievement.

---

[25] See Johan Huizinga, *Homo Ludens: A Study of the Play Element in Culture.*

[26] Ibid., p. 12. The effects of secrets and the role of play will be discussed later.

[27] "The Inferior Function," in *Psychotherapy*, p. 142.

[28] *C.G. Jung Letters*, vol. 1, p. 60.

[29] "The Religious Dimension of Analysis," in *Psychotherapy*, p. 200.

The psychology of C.G. Jung is a lived psychology, concerned with the life of individuals, particularly in the realm of self-knowledge. This is not to be understood as the knowledge possessed by the ego. It is more nuanced. The ego is required to become strong enough to witness and receive expressions from the unconscious, by means of the transcendent function, thereby developing a relationship with it. Jung notes that "constant observation pays the unconscious a tribute that more or less guarantees its cooperation."[30] He considers this attention to be crucial:

> It is, in fact, one of the most important tasks of psychic hygiene to pay continual attention to the symptomatology of unconscious contents and processes, for the good reason that the conscious mind is always in danger of becoming one-sided, of keeping to well-worn paths and getting stuck in blind alleys. The complementary and compensating function of the unconscious ensures that these dangers, which are especially great in neurosis, can in some measure be avoided.[31]

Through this process the personality, and therefore the experience of living, is deepened. Analytical psychology is concerned with a person's nature and the realization of meaning.

Jung's view of the psyche and its processes is not schematic, but rather has as its root metaphor the imagery of nature. At the beginning of his autobiography, he describes his basic understanding of human beings and their destiny in images from nature:

> Life has always seemed to me like a plant that lives on its rhizome. Its true life is invisible, hidden in the rhizome. The part that appears above ground lasts only a single summer. Then it withers away. . . . Yet I have never lost a sense of something that lives and endures underneath the eternal flux. What we see is the blossom, which passes. The rhizome remains.[32]

This imagery refers not only to the beginning and end of a person's life. It is also an image of the source of all psychic processes. They do not come from the blossom. Rather, the blossom depends on the stem

---

[30] *Aion,* CW 9ii, par.40.

[31] Ibid.

[32] *Memories, Dreams, Reflections,* p. 4.

which comes from the rhizome, the root, the part hidden underground, unseen. Psychologically this can be considered the unconscious. Thus phenomena that emerge from the rhizome are necessary for the blossoming of the individuation process.

Self-knowledge, Individuation and Analysis

Individuation is a natural process but sometimes it is blocked, or stunted, so that the personality cannot develop. Therefore the individual cannot blossom and is cut off from his or her own psychic soil and life force. This eventually becomes a form of psychic death which can be the source of deep suffering. Some people think that if they can just soldier on, eventually everything will be all right. Others think that by self-examination they can figure out their problems.

In general, there is a common attitude that if one can identify the problem, a solution can be found. This is only sometimes true. For the most part, problem solving is an effort by the ego which does not include the difficult, puzzling material from the unconscious in its deliberations. The ego also tends to busy itself by labeling everything, often in the hope of solving problems. "We are so used to living out of a conceptual context that we spare ourselves the encounter with raw facts."[33]

Marie-Louise von Franz describes the limitations of these efforts:

One sees people . . . who know nothing about the reality of the unconscious but who can spend hours and hours thinking in their ego about their ego. Sometimes these people come to analysis with a tremendous consciousness of their ego character. They do know their own ego amazingly well. Of course nobody knows it completely, but such people have really honestly tried to think about themselves. Even nowadays most people still think that to become conscious of oneself means to reflect on one's own personality, just to think and brood . . . . This is why people assume that analysis and psychology are all egocentric and that one should . . . rather help hungry mankind. But that is not what we do in analysis. To think about the ego would be completely sterile.[34]

---

[33] Edward F. Edinger, *The Aion Lectures,* p. 11.

[34] *Alchemical Active Imagination,* p. 70.

Individuation is an important concept in Jungian psychology and also in the growth of the personality, whether one is in personal analysis or not. Jung writes of it as follows:

> In general, it is the process by which individual beings are formed and differentiated; in particular, it is the development of the psychological *individual* as a being distinct from the general, collective psychology. Individuation, therefore, is a process of *differentiation,* having for its goal the development of the individual personality.
>
>   . . . As the individual is not just a single, separate being, but by his very existence presupposes a collective relationship, it follows that the process of individuation must lead to more intense and broader collective relationships and not to isolation.[35]

A certain minimal adaptation to collective functioning is a precursor to the individuation process. The reason, writes Jung, is that "if a plant is to unfold its specific nature to the full, it must first be able to grow in the soil in which it is planted."[36]

The work of individuation requires the humility to recognize that there is much one does not know in relation to oneself, and the willingness to consider what is revealed by the unconscious. In this enterprise the ego's narrow field of vision is expanded so that one's consciousness is increased. Another necessary requirement is the capacity to weather the tension of opposites. Inevitably situations will arise that are in conflict with one's habitual way of being and self-understanding. This type of conflict cannot be resolved by the rationality of the ego. It can only be suffered until eventually a new understanding dawns so that another direction becomes apparent.

It is not an easy path. The ego has to be or become strong enough to receive the variety and apparent strangeness of material which the unconscious may reveal. It is also important to honor the process by thoughtfully living it. There is as well an ethical dimension: to give something of oneself to the world out of one's own authentic being. Such contributions made to the collective must come from one's true gifts

---

[35] "Definitions," *Psychological Types,* CW 6, pars. 757f.

[36] Ibid., par. 760.

rather than merely conforming to expectations associated with general rules and social norms.

Individuation is not a particularly systematic process, nor is it a final state which one attains, never to be challenged again. It is a work forever in progress. As Jung tells us:

> The goal is important only as an idea; the essential thing is the *opus* which leads to the goal: *that* is the goal of a lifetime. In its attainment "left and right" are united, and conscious and unconscious work in harmony.[37]

Analysis fosters this process. It is like an inner mystery school. The knowledge gained comes from the unconscious as it reveals itself. Learning to relate to this material can be very moving. This is the beginning of the effort toward self-knowledge, in the interest of discovering answers to the question, "Who am I, really?" The discovery includes not only *who* but *what* one is. It becomes apparent that each of us is embedded somewhere that is not identical with the subjective ego. There is a dawning awareness of the breathtaking mystery at work within. The apostle Paul seems to recognize this when he says, "You are a letter of Christ . . . written not with ink but with the Spirit of the living God, not on tablets of stone but on tablets of human hearts." (2 Cor. 3:3)[38]

There may also come an appreciation *that* one is. The anonymous author of *The Book of Privy Counseling* urges us to contemplate this:

> I grant that to realize what you are demands the effort of your intelligence in a good deal of thought and subtle introspection. . . . Remember that you also possess an innate ability to know *that you are*, and that you can experience this without any special natural or acquired genius.[39]

This contemplation brings riches to the interior life.

> Happy is [one], who enriches [the] interior life with a loving, delicate, spiritual knowledge that far transcends all the knowledge of natural or ac-

---

[37] "The Psychology of the Transference," *The Practice of Psychotherapy,* CW 16, par. 400.

[38] Biblical references are to the New Revised Standard Version, unless otherwise noted.

[39] Quoted in Moore and Moore, eds., *The Neighborhood of IS*, p. 28.

quired genius. Far better this wisdom and an ease in this delicate, refined interior work than the gain of gold or silver.[40]

A similar valuing of this effort is found in the Gnostic *Gospel of Thomas: Unearthing the Lost Words of Jesus:*

> If those who lead you say, "Look, the kingdom is in heaven," then the birds of heaven will precede you. If they say, "It is in the sea," then the fish will precede you. Rather, the kingdom is within you and outside you. When you know yourselves, you will be known, and you will know you are children of the living father. But if you do not know yourselves, you live in poverty and you yourselves are the poverty.[41]

It is a process of relatedness. Gradually one connects with previously unknown facets of the personality that enrich or restart the flow of life. One then becomes sensitive to the ebb and flow of one's energy. Without such a sensitivity, it is easy to violate the laws of one's being. But with it, one begins to live in accord with one's unique nature.

Again we are encouraged by the writer of *The Book of Privy Counseling,* who urges us to "remain whole and recollected in the depths of your being as often as you can."[42]

Individuation is a process of revelation, assimilation and transformation. Often problems are outgrown, rather than cured or solved, in this journey toward wholeness. Jung writes:

> It leads in the end to that distant goal which may perhaps have been the first urge to life: the complete actualization of the whole human being, that is, individuation.[43]

---

[40] Ibid.

[41] John Dart and Ray Riegert, eds., *The Gospel of Thomas,* Saying 3, p. 15.

[42] Quoted in Moore and Moore, eds., *The Neighborhood of IS,* p. 72.

[43] "The Practical Use of Dream-Analysis," *The Practice of Psychotherapy,* CW 16, par. 352.

Figure 3. Walled garden of fruits and flowers.
(From an illuminated Bible manuscript, 13th century)

2

Personal Reflections

A cultivated garden contains all the elements of instinctual life and death, light and dark, creation and destruction, found in the wild. But here nature invites an appreciative partnership. The garden is a container for the elemental life force, a container within which we may witness the wonders of nature. This can be a source of pleasure, inspiration and even healing. There are many forms of gardens in all cultures. In Japan there are gardens of transcendence; gardens of rapture in Italy; of reflection in the Islamic world. England has created gardens of transition, whereas New York city has gardens of refuge and Russia ones of inspiration. There are gardens of enchantment in India. Each type of garden evokes a particular inner response.

In addition to physical gardens, perhaps even more potent are the ones that live in the imagination:

> Deep within each of us lies a garden. An intensely personal place, this landscape grows from a rich blend of ingredients—imagination, memory, character, and dreams—that combine in wonderful ways in our innermost selves. Throughout most of our lives, this garden remains hidden from view save for brief glimpses during moments spent daydreaming or in quiet contemplation.[44]

> [It is] as much a state of mind as it is an actual place. It exists because you discover a place of beauty that feels set apart in space and time.[45]

Gardens have been places of delight for me since childhood. Some of my earliest, most cherished memories originate there. I always knew that. It took longer to realize that the garden is a potent symbol for the psyche and the individuation process. Early in my analytic journey I had a compelling dream:

---

[44] Julie Moir Messervy, *The Inward Garden,* p. 11.
[45] Ibid., p. 19.

I had been on a trip. I did not call home. On the last night, there was a party which was very lively and successful. I realized that the woman who had created this party was not present. When I asked about her, someone showed me where she was. Apparently she lived in a little hut, a sort of garage, in the garden behind the house.

I walked down a long path in the garden. There were flowers and trees blossoming everywhere. There were tiny lights all around, in the midst of the plants. When I found the woman, I was shocked to discover that she was locked in a cage. She was a radiantly beautiful black woman. She looked at me intensely and said, "It's my party!" as she gestured to the house and then to the garden.

This was my first meeting in dreams with the figure I call the Dark Woman. She is a numinous presence who still appears from time to time, bringing a sense of orientation because of the feeling of grace which she imparts. This feeling is "a kind of transformation of consciousness that takes place without any effort on the part of the individual who experiences it."[46]

Though mysterious, the Dark Woman has a life-giving effect. Every spring when I am privileged to witness the miraculous unfolding of nature, I can hear her saying, "It's my party!" I believe it was this initial encounter with the Dark Woman that revealed the garden to me as a numinous, living symbol.

As a child I had a great love for my grandparents' house and garden. They lived in a very large, elegant Victorian house on a tree-lined street in a small village. The main garden was behind the house. There were flowers, lawn, a vegetable garden, and nearby, a tool shed. Beyond that, there was wild land—fields, then dense forest. It struck me even then how quickly the cultivated garden of my grandparents gave way to what seemed to me to be untamed nature. How narrow was the boundary between one and the other! This was the order of the universe as I perceived it then. Now, when I consider this landscape symbolically, it is still meaningful.

My grandparents' house and garden have become a model of the psy-

---

[46] Moore and Moore, eds., *The Neighborhood of IS,* p. 14.

che for me. The garden represents the personal unconscious. Jung distinguishes between the personal and the collective unconscious. Based on his experience, he considered the personal unconscious to comprise "all the acquisitions of personal life, everything forgotten, repressed, subliminally perceived, thought, felt."[47] It also contains "sense-perceptions that were not strong enough to reach consciousness, and finally, contents that are not yet ripe for consciousness."[48]

The forest and all that is beyond the garden is like the collective unconscious. This is a structural layer of the human psyche containing inherited elements, distinct from the personal unconscious. It contains "the whole spiritual heritage of mankind's evolution, born anew in the brain structure of every individual."[49] The contents of the collective unconscious are inherited, not personal acquisitions. The contents include "the mythological associations, the motifs and images that can spring up anew anytime, anywhere, independently of historical tradition or migration."[50]

The front of the house with its beautiful lawn and stately trees facing the village seems to me to be like the persona, which Jung thought of as "a functional complex that comes into existence for reasons of adaptation or personal convenience."[51] It is usually via the persona that one meets the outer world. Often it is confused with one's true identity and individuality. Jung writes:

> Fundamentally the persona is nothing real: it is a compromise between individual and society as to what a man should appear to be. He takes a name, earns a title, exercises a function, he is this or that. In a certain sense all this is real, yet in relation to the essential individuality of the person concerned it is only a secondary reality.[52]

---

[47] "Definitions," *Psychological Types,* CW 6, par. 842.

[48] "The Personal and the Collective Unconscious," *Two Essays on Analytical Psychology,* CW 7, par. 103.

[49] "The Structure of the Psyche," *The Structure and Dynamics of the Psyche,* CW 8, par. 342.

[50] "Definitions," *Psychological Types,* CW 6, par. 842.

[51] Ibid., par. 801.

[52] "The Persona as a Segment of the Collective Psyche," *Two Essays,* CW 7, par. 246.

Nevertheless the persona facilitates social interactions by functioning as a protective covering as well as adapting to collective norms in society. It helps a person to meet the world.

The house itself represents the ego in this model of the psyche that developed from my musings upon my grandparents' home and my experience there. Jung says, "By ego I understand a complex of ideas which constitutes the centre of my field of consciousness and appears to possess a high degree of continuity and identity."[53]

In the center of the house was a magnificent stained glass window, situated so that radiant, colorful light filled the central hall. When I was a child this window filled me with awe, and at times fear. It seemed to be a holy mystery. I could never bring myself to speak about it to anyone. I developed a ritual which enabled me to pass close to it when necessary. I imagined the presence of some Other reality in its vicinity. Now I think of it as an image of the Self, the timeless aspect of the psyche.

Jung considers the Self to be supraordinate to the ego, corresponding to what the alchemists describe as the "One and Indivisible that cannot be reduced to anything else and is at the same time a Universal."[54] Elsewhere he writes:

> The ego stands to the self as the moved to the mover, or as object to subject, because the determining factors which radiate out from the self surround the ego on all sides and are therefore supraordinate to it. The self, like the unconscious, is an *a priori* existent out of which the ego evolves.[55]

When the ego is touched by the Self, the experience is numinous. Gradually, in the individuation process, a new center of the personality develops as the ego and the Self come into closer relationship. The personality is enlarged. This process involves certain risks, risks I clearly sensed as a child when I was in the presence of what I now consider to be a symbol of the Self, namely the stained glass window in my grandparents' home.

---

[53] "Definitions," *Psychological Types,* CW 6, par. 706.

[54] "Psychotherapy Today," *The Practice of Psychotherapy,* CW 16, par. 220.

[55] "Transformation Symbolism in the Mass," *Psychology and Religion,* CW 11, par. 391.

My grandparents died when I was ten years old. I never returned to their home again. Yet these images have always fed my imagination. At first it was in a general way. Now they have become organized into a framework for an understanding of the structure of the psyche that nourishes my analytic work.

Some years ago I attended a workshop on the symbolic landscape. First we drew images from childhood; next, from our present life. Then we placed the second drawing over the first and held them to the light. Looking at these two pictures in this way, I discovered that my bed was situated precisely in the midst of my grandparents' garden. This was another defining moment of recognition regarding the centrality of this symbol for my own experience of wholeness. No wonder I have had so many garden dreams over the years: my bed is there!

For years I had another memory mingling with these. It was of a different garden, hidden away somewhere, a world unto itself. I remembered it as beautiful, mysterious, secluded, quiet, possibly even secret. Yet when I entered it there was an intimate feeling of being welcome. "Where *is* this place?" I often wondered, perplexed. There was satisfaction in recalling the story of *The Secret Garden*. My fanciful memories were mirrored there. Nevertheless, I did not reject the possibility that a garden existed somewhere in the outer world that corresponded to the one I either remembered or imagined. Since I had not located it geographically, it lived within me as a personal, secret garden. It was a source of solace, inspiration, as well as slight yearning. It became a sort of anchor for my inner solitude, a cherished place in my imagination for meditative reflection.

Years passed before I returned to the village where my grandparents had lived. Eventually, after my parents had also died, I ventured to return in order to renew contact with some relatives who still lived there. It was a beautiful summer day. My uncle asked if I would like to visit Mrs. McIntyre's garden. In a spirit of cooperation, but without great expectations, I replied that yes, I would.

Mrs. McIntyre was an elderly, highly respected lady in the village. She had been a friend of my grandparents and their children, one of whom was my mother. We were very pleased to meet each other again. We walked down the stone path outside her front door. It was bordered on both sides by lush flowers. I exclaimed how beautiful the garden was. "We have not reached it yet," she replied. Then, turning a corner, we entered a luxurious shade garden formed by a cathedral of trees. There was another stone path forming the central aisle, with masses of flowers blooming on both sides despite the shade. This struck me as spectacular. Once again, I expressed my delight in the garden. Again I was told, "We have not reached it yet!"

Eventually we walked under an arbor laden with pink roses. Thereupon we entered the enchanted garden of my memory! Here it was, entirely hidden from the world, surrounded by huge, old trees. Within the circle of this garden there was a special radiance. Mrs. McIntyre had faithfully tended it for the past fifty years. A cornerstone of her life, the garden was an essential part of her spiritual path. This was a moment of breathtaking discovery for me. It took my breath away to realize that the cherished garden of my memory and imagination existed in the outer world. It was a wonder to contemplate this elderly woman's loving care and loyalty to one place.

I often think of Mrs. McIntyre and her garden as a metaphor for the analytic process. To me she is an image of "the faithful gardener," the person who faithfully tends the garden of the psyche.[56] She also represents the feminine aspect of the ego in a harmonious relationship with the Self. Growth in the analytic process requires careful attention to dreams and other unconscious material, to feelings, to the conditions of life, so that the experience and possibly the meaning of these may be incorporated into one's personality and mode of being in the world. This is often a long, slow process. The relationship between analyst and analysand helps to provide focus and stability during the course of the analysis. But for an entire life, it is a person's relationship to the inner garden of the psyche which will give continuity and enrichment.

It is deeply instructive to contemplate this image of the wise old woman carefully and patiently attending to the particular details of her

---

[56] See Clarissa Pinkola Estes, *The Faithful Gardener.*

garden, so that in the fullness of time it comes to fruition. It is also an inspiration to me when I work as an analyst with individuals who are starting to engage with their inner world.

Jung uses the metaphor of gardening to describe analysis, comparing individuals to trees. He is convinced that "the individual is the carrier of life," and that "we have served life's purpose if one tree at least succeeds in bearing fruit, though a thousand others remain barren." Since the purpose of analysis is the development of the individual, says Jung, "our efforts will follow nature's own striving to bring life to the fullest possible fruition in each individual, for only in the individual can life fulfil its meaning."[57]

Not everyone is called to this work. But if one does become engaged with it, then the process yields its own satisfactions. The author of *The Cloud of Unknowing* describes the circular relationship a person has with the work, which he understands as a sacred process of approaching the inner solitude where one experiences the ineffable divine majesty in one's own human experience. He reflects that

> the ability to do this work is inherently contained in the work itself so that whoever feels this work is thereby enabled to do it. . . . To the degree that you . . . desire it, you have that much of it. . . . And yet it is not a matter of . . . desire, but something . . . that stirs you to desire.[58]

Progress depends upon an aptitude, fuelled by inner stirrings of desire in partnership with dedication, rather than by utilitarian motives. The writer of *The Cloud of Unknowing* attributes this to God: "Trust . . . that it is . . . God who is stirring your will and your desire . . . with no special devices being used, neither by Him nor by you."[59] With no loss of awe, this could also be called the stirring of the Self within the individual.

Some years ago Mrs. McIntyre died. The garden has been abandoned. It suffers from the loss of the animating love that nurtured it for decades. It has fallen into a fallow period which now looks like chaos. Will it have

---

[57] "Psychotherapy Today," *The Practice of Psychotherapy,* CW 16, par. 229.
[58] Quoted in Moore and Moore, eds., *The Neighborhood of IS,* p. 78.
[59] Ibid.

a future? That remains to be seen. But on another level it lives in the hearts and souls of those who treasured it, those of us who had the privilege of experiencing it. It shines in my memory, a beloved symbol in the landscape of my soul, inexhaustible. As Jung says,

> A symbol does not define or explain; it points beyond itself to a meaning that is darkly divined yet still beyond our grasp, and cannot be adequately expressed in the familiar words of our language.[60]

The symbolic world in my dreams gradually revealed a more specific path for me in relation to this material. In order to illustrate the delicate but distinct guidance that can be given from the inner depths, I will recount several dreams that were given to me. After the discoveries described above, I ventured to reread *The Secret Garden*. I was stirred once again by the story. My interest became more focused. I wondered if this symbol was a vehicle for further distillation in my process. I even wondered if I might ultimately write about it. Then I had this dream:

> I went to visit my friend, who had visitors. I joined the group in the living room. Everyone was discussing the subject of gardening. It was compellingly interesting to me. It was like recognizing something very big. There was a lot of energy connected with it.
>
> Then I was at the C.G. Jung Institute in Zurich for a lecture. It was very crowded but I managed to find a place to sit. A man came to sit beside me. He was very kind. There was a real kinship bond between us even though we did not know each other. First he put his arms around me. Then he put his hands on my head in a loving way. I welcomed this because my head was really hurting. His gesture was a relief and a comfort to me.
>
> Someone announced that we needed special lights—sort of like Christmas tree lights. I was perplexed and dismayed. Why should we be expected to have such lights with us all of a sudden? A woman said she had some. She proceeded to set them up efficiently and plug them in. The man who was sitting with me objected to this mechanical procedure. So he and I left. We went down to the basement.
>
> The Dark Woman was there with her husband and their baby whom they seemed to love greatly. At first I walked past them on my way to

---

[60] "Spirit and Life," *The Structure and Dynamics of the Psyche*, CW 8, par. 644.

somewhere else, not sure where. But the man I was with told me to stop and speak with them. So I went back. When I spoke with them they were very pleased. They became radiant. I felt joy. The baby, who was a handsome little boy, became interested in me and I in him.

The prospect of exploring gardening and *The Secret Garden* seemed to constellate Eros in the depths. This expressed itself in the dream with several healing encounters. The first was the fellowship I found at the house of my friend. The next was with the man who says "No" to the mechanical, systematic approach to learning. This is not for me. Rather my path is to accept his healing touch and to go to the basement with him, to the warmth and darkness there. In so doing I meet the Dark Woman with her family. Seeing them was to be in the presence of feelings, feminine intuition and mystery.

My animus, or inner masculine, wanted me to find this light which emanated from the Dark Holy Family in the depths, rather than from Christmas light bulbs. The love and sensuality of the Dark Woman with her family radiate their own light and vitality. It seemed that the garden was to be that place of mystery and discovery for me.

I pondered this dream, appreciating its radiance, letting its energy pulse with its own rhythm. A year later there were two further dreams that crystallized my desire to write on this subject. Here is the first:

I went to the bookstore at the University of Toronto to find some books but everything had been changed. In the place where the books had been there were now computers. I was dismayed and disoriented. A saucy young man told me where the books were now located but his directions were unintelligible to me. Then to my surprise he offered to show me where they were. When we got there I was delighted to find that it was a café and library with lots of plants, light and air, and many spacious tables. I thought it was a wonderful discovery since it was hidden away and very quiet. It seemed to be a secret place, a kind of secret garden.

The second dream, really only a fragment, occurred one month later: "A very beautiful older woman, along with various other people, were having a meal together. This woman was radiantly attractive." When I awoke I made the following entry in my journal:

Bliss this morning! I wonder if I might write about *The Secret Garden* as a symbol of revelation and renewal in analysis and the individuation process? I would love to use the story as the central, organizing element in an exploration of all the themes I have been mulling over—Eros, renewal, sacrifice, transcendence, masculine, feminine, youth, age, death and rebirth. This prospect gives me a feeling of deep contentment. I wonder if it will work?

The following spring I began writing what would become this book. I wondered how to approach the material, how to organize my thoughts and discoveries. Once again the dream world gave me directions, which I have tried to follow to the best of my ability. Here is the dream:

> I was having supervision with a woman I did not know. She was very elegant and lovely, all dressed in white. After the session she disappeared but I stayed in her home for a while. Then it seemed that a party was about to begin, so I stayed. . . . The woman had prepared a lot of food and was circulating among the guests. She was very refined. She wore a beautiful dress with some lovely jewelry and an evening bag.
>
> Later I was walking down the street with her. She mentioned *The Secret Garden*. I was excited to hear what she had to say. I thought it was quite insightful. I told her I was going to be writing about that. She wanted to be involved somehow. . . . Then I made a long descent to a very strange, fascinating place. It seemed to be a dwelling from a totally different culture. Even though this place was deep underground, inside a mountain, there was still lots of light and air. Huge logs formed part of the roof and sides. I was particularly intrigued by all the stoves that were in this place. They were old, wood-burning stoves, not large, but nice little ones like those we had at the cottage when I was a teenager. Fires were burning in each of these old, pot-bellied stoves.

The elegant, refined woman could help me to some extent with her ideas, interest, social grace, but the real energy is in the stoves, burning inside the mountain, away from the known world. Somehow it is important to be in touch with the two worlds—the upper and the lower, intellectual as well as the emotional fire in the depth. It seemed to be an encouraging dream of connections and reconnections.

The duality presented in the dream is also an aspect of nature and, therefore, of the garden as well as the psyche. The psychic totality of each individual partakes of this duality. Analyst Françoise O'Kane writes:

> The Self is given, is unquestionable and unfathomable, and it manifests an ambiguous nature, both benevolent and nefarious. Further, far from being only an ordering principle, the Self, like the sacred, is related to chaos; it pertains to nature and to the origins of humanity. It is a powerful entity which thinking and reason cannot simply structure and explain.[61]

Acknowledgment of the chaos that is part of nature and personal growth enables the ego "to find a better grounding and to relate differently to the dark aspects of the unconscious."[62] This grounding makes life more complete than if it is viewed with vague or too optimistic generalizations.

Sometimes it is initiation by life's most bitter suffering in the depths of apparent chaos that leads to the genuine gift of spiritual awareness and growth, as we shall see in the story of *The Secret Garden*. We may wonder sometimes, "What is that which can never die?"[63] The answer appears to be:

> It is that faithful force that is born into us, that one that is greater than us, that calls new seed to the open and battered and barren places, so that we can be resown.[64]

Through this symbol of the garden I realized that the wholeness about which we speak in Jungian psychology is a constant process of cycles, balance, attention, movement. As every gardener knows, it is not only the blossom or the harvest that is important. It is all the phases of the garden—the seasons, the new growth, the decay, the fallow periods; the planting and waiting; the partnership with nature. All of these matter. There is also the vital element of chance—which seeds take hold of life, which ones die; when the sun shines or the rain comes.

---

[61] *Sacred Chaos,* p. 48.

[62] Ibid., p. 49.

[63] Estes, *The Faithful Gardener,* p. 66.

[64] Ibid., pp. 66f.

Joseph Campbell, in the series of video-taped interviews with Bill Moyers which became the book entitled *The Power of Myth,* speaks about the crucial role of chance in life. He was asked, "Is there anything in your life that did not occur by chance?" Campbell replied:

> The ultimate backing for life is chance—the chance that your parents met, for example! Chance, or what might seem to be chance, is the means through which life is realized. The problem is not to blame or explain but to handle the life that arises.[65]

"Chance" is the name of the gardener in the novel *Being There* by Jerzy Kosinski. Sitting in his garden, Chance muses about the variety of forces at work within it:

> The wind, mindless of direction, intermittently swayed the bushes and the trees. The city's dust settled evenly, darkening the flowers, which waited patiently to be rinsed by the rain and dried by the sunshine. And yet, at the peak of its bloom, the garden was its own graveyard. Under every tree and bush lay rotten trunks and disintegrated and decomposing roots. It was hard to know which was more important: the garden's surface or the graveyard from which it grew and into which it was constantly lapsing.[66]

All of this is the wholeness of the garden, nature and the psyche: above and below; light and dark; growth and decay; order and chaos; life and death. This is also the interest of Jungian psychology. It is concerned with all aspects of life. There is sometimes confusion about this. Wholeness and individuation are not forms of perfection or states of nirvana. A perfectionist attitude strives for the attainment of a purely positive state, forgetting that the wholeness of human beings includes pain, failure, laziness, doubt, guilt, paradox and unconsciousness, as well as joy, creativity, consciousness and fulfillment. Such is the variegated spectrum of wholeness.

In the journey toward wholeness, one is urged beyond the confining aspects of that which is already understood, to "a realm of experiencing and knowing which is beyond what our current map can accurately

---

[65] *The Power of Myth,* p. 203.
[66] *Being There,* p. 4.

communicate."[67] It is "an experience of incomparable value,"[68] which imbues life with a unique vitality.

The cultivation of one's individuality in analysis, as in gardening, requires a certain receptivity so that when the excess has been released, "something happens within the Inner Solitude which might be described as 'grace'—a gift from the Source of All."[69] Then by means of the "stillness of all reasoning powers . . . [and] by a rejection of all knowledge [one] possesses a knowledge that exceeds understanding."[70]

An example of the ultimate value of this stillness in the inner solitude is apparent in the following description of an elderly doctor in Solzhenitsyn's novel *Cancer Ward*:

> He had to take frequent rests nowadays. His body demanded this chance to recoup its strength and with the same urgency his inner self demanded silent contemplation free of external sounds, conversations, thoughts of work, free of everything that made him a doctor. Particularly after the death of his wife, his inner consciousness had seemed to crave a pure transparency. It was just this sort of silent immobility, without planned or even floating thoughts, which gave him a sense of purity and fulfillment.
>
> At such moments an image of the whole meaning of existence—his own during the long past and the short future ahead, that of his late wife, of his young granddaughter, and of everyone in the world—came to mind. The image he saw did not seem to be embodied in the work or activity which occupied them, which they believed was central to their lives, and by which they were known to others. The meaning of existence was to preserve unspoiled, undisturbed and undistorted the image of eternity with which each person is born. Like a silver moon in a calm, still pond.[71]

In the sanctuary of the secret garden, there is a temenos for explorations that can engender the flowering of the personality, an awakening to the fullness of life from the core of one's being.

---

[67] Moore and Moore, eds., *The Neighborhood of IS*, p. 18.

[68] Ibid., p. 29.

[69] Ibid., p. 80.

[70] Ibid., p. 81.

[71] *Cancer Ward*, p. 427.

Figure 4. "Mary pushed back the door which opened slowly . . ."

3
Summary of *The Secret Garden*

Mary Lennox was a disagreeable, demanding young girl who had been born in India to English parents.

> Her father had held a position under the English government and had always been busy and ill himself, and her mother had been a great beauty who cared only to go to parties and amuse herself with gay people.[72]

Certainly her mother had not welcomed a baby girl into her life. As soon as she was born Mary was handed over to the care of an ayah (servant) who was made to understand that if she wished to please the Mem Sahib she must keep the child out of sight as much as possible. All the servants obeyed Mary, letting her have her own way in everything, so that "by the time she was six years old she was as tyrannical and selfish a little pig as ever lived."

When Mary was nine, her parents died in a cholera epidemic, leaving her an orphan.

> The cholera had broken out in its most fatal form and people were dying like flies. . . . During the confusion and bewilderment . . . Mary hid herself in the nursery and was forgotten by everyone. Nobody thought of her, nobody wanted her.

When she was eventually found, Mary became the ward of her uncle, Mr. Archibald Craven, a wealthy, reclusive man whose home was a vast estate named Misselthwaite Manor, located on the English moors. With these radical developments in her young life, Mary began to wonder why she had never seemed to belong to anyone, even when her father and mother were alive.

---

[72] All quotations and extracts are from Frances Hodgson Burnett, *The Secret Garden*. Page references are not given here as there have been many editions in different formats since it was first published in 1911.

Other children seemed to belong to their fathers and mothers, but she had never seemed to really be any one's little girl. She had had servants, and food and clothes, but no one had taken any notice of her. She did not know that this was because she was a disagreeable child; but then, of course, she did not know she was disagreeable. She often thought that other people were, but she did not know that she was so herself.

After her long voyage from India, Mary was met in London by Mrs. Medlock, the housekeeper at Misselthwaite Manor.

Mary did not like her at all, but as she very seldom liked people there was nothing remarkable in that; besides which it was very evident Mrs. Medlock did not think much of her.

Mrs. Medlock informed her:

You are going to a queer place. . . . Not but that it's a grand big place in a gloomy way, and Mr. Craven is proud of it in his way—and that's gloomy enough too. The house is six hundred years old and it's on the edge of the moor, and there's near a hundred rooms in it, though most of them's shut up and locked.

Mary listened with a little interest because it was all so new to her. "But she did not intend to look as if she were interested. That was one of her unhappy, disagreeable ways. So she sat still."

They traveled from London by train to Thwaite Station where there was still a long drive across the moor before reaching Misselthwaite Manor. Mary pondered all that she had heard from Mrs. Medlock.

She was not at all a timid child and she was not exactly frightened, but she felt that there was no knowing what might happen in a house with a hundred rooms nearly all shut up—a house standing on the edge of a moor.

"What is a moor?" she asked. [She could not see anything since it was dark.] "It's not the sea is it?" she wondered. Mrs. Medlock answered, "No, not it . . . Nor it isn't fields nor mountains, it's just miles and miles and miles of wild land that nothing grows on but heather and gorse and broom, and nothing lives on but wild ponies and sheep."

Mary thought it even sounded like the sea but was told that it was "the wind blowing through the bushes." She concluded to herself, "I don't like it." They finally arrived at their destination. As Mary stood on the stone floor, "she looked a very small, odd little black figure, and she felt as small and lost and odd as she looked."

There was a retinue of servants at Misselthwaite Manor to take care of the one hundred rooms and extensive grounds. Since Mr. Craven, the master, was rarely there, the responsibility for managing the household belonged to the redoubtable Mrs. Medlock, the head housekeeper.

> She was the kind of woman who would "stand no nonsense from the young ones." . . . She had a comfortable, well-paid place as a housekeeper at Misselthwaite Manor and the only way in which she could keep it was to do at once what Mr. Archibald Craven told her to do. She never dared to ask a question.

Mr. Craven himself was rarely at home because he traveled almost constantly in an effort to numb his grief following the untimely death of his beloved wife, Lilias, ten years earlier.

Mary is oriented to her new home by Mrs. Medlock who gives her the following instructions:

> You needn't expect to see him, because ten to one you won't. And you mustn't expect that there will be people to talk to you. You'll have to play about and look after yourself. You'll be told what rooms you can go into and what rooms you're to keep out of. There's gardens enough. But when you are in the house don't go wandering and poking about. Mr. Craven won't have it.

Mercifully, Mary is assigned a young woman named Martha as her maidservant. Martha is a natural, spontaneous girl who loves the English moors. She says, "I wouldn't live away from the moor for anything." She is the eldest in a large, poor Yorkshire family. She is practical, capable, straightforward and resilient. She teaches Mary many important lessons just by being herself. One is how to get dressed. Until she met Martha it had never occurred to Mary that this was a skill she might learn. In India her ayah had always dressed her.

When Mary inquires, "Who is going to dress me?" Martha is dismayed and asks incredulously, "I mean can't you put on your own clothes?" When it is apparent that that is the situation, Martha matter-offactly asserts, "Well . . . it's time tha' should learn. . . . It'll do thee good to wait on thysen a bit."

If Martha had been a well-trained, fine young lady's maid, she would have been more subservient. But she was a vivacious Yorkshire lass "who had been brought up in a moorland cottage with a swarm of little brothers and sisters who never dreamed of doing anything but wait on themselves."

Martha chatted freely, "but Mary only listened to her coldly and wondered at her freedom of manner." She had no interest in anything or anyone at first. But gradually a change came over her. As Martha rattled on in her good-tempered, homely way, Mary began to notice what she was saying. She even began to have insights about herself. In comparison to what she hears from Martha, Mary realizes: "People never like me and I never like people."

Left to her own devices, Mary becomes curious about the world around her. First she takes an interest in the weather, the air and the moor, which she learns about from Martha who encourages her to go outside to play. When Mary asks, "Who will go with me?" Martha replies that she will have to go by herself and learn to play. She mentions her brother Dickon who finds the moor, along with all its plants and animal inhabitants, so fascinating that he can spend all day there. This piques Mary's curiosity to start exploring. Martha also tells her that there are many gardens on the estate, one of which has been locked for ten years, ever since Mr. Craven's wife died.

> Mary could not help thinking about the garden which no one had been into for ten years. She wondered what it would look like and whether there were any flowers still alive in it.

So Mary starts to investigate the grounds of the estate. In the course of her explorations, she makes the acquaintance of Ben Weatherstaff, the elderly gardener. He is just as gruff as she is ornery. They have an affinity which enables them to develop a friendship of sorts. Ben tells Mary that they are quite similar. He sums it up by saying, "We've got the same nasty tempers." Mary was shocked. "This was plain speaking, and Mary Lennox had never heard the truth about herself in her life."

Ben also introduces her to his friend the robin who lives in the garden. He tells her that the robin was lonely when he was younger.

> Mary went a step nearer to the robin and looked at him very hard. "I'm lonely," she said. She had not known before that this was one of the things that made her sour and cross. She seemed to find it out when the robin looked at her and she looked at the robin.

She begins to see both herself and others. She also discovers that she can like people and they in turn can become fond of her.

At the same time, Mary's curiosity and imagination are inflamed by the walled area, overgrown with vines, that does not appear to have any door. She cannot accept this perplexing situation, but neither can she discover any point of entry.

One night Mary and Martha were sitting cosily by the fire in her room while the wind blew eerily across the moors. Martha said, "Listen to th' wind wutherin' round the house. . . . You could bare stand upon the moor if you was out on it tonight."

> Mary did not know what "wutherin' " meant until she listened, and then she understood. It must mean that hollow shuddering sort of roar which rushed round and round the house as if the giant no one could see was buffeting it and beating at the walls and windows to try to break in. But one knew he could not get in, and somehow it made one feel very safe and warm inside a room with a red coal fire.

Mary was feeling safe and cozy for the first time in her young life.

This had been the day when Mary felt quite sure she had found the locked garden.

> This gave her so much to think of that she began to be quite interested and feel that she was not sorry that she had come to Misselthwaite Manor. . . . The fact was that the fresh wind from the moor had begun to blow the cobwebs out of her young brain and to waken her up a little.

As they chatted by the fire, listening to the wind, Martha revealed,

> There's lots o' things in this place that's not to be talked over. That's Mr. Craven's orders. . . . But for th' garden he wouldn't be like he is. It was Mrs. Craven's garden that she made when first they were married an' she

just loved it, an' they used to 'tend the flowers themselves. An' none o' th' gardeners was ever let to go in. Him an' her used to go in an' shut th' door an' stay there hours an' hours, readin' and talkin'. An' she was just a bit of a girl an' there was an old tree with a branch bent like a seat on it. An' she made roses grow over it an' she used to sit there. But one day when she was sittin' there th' branch broke an' she fell on th' ground an' was hurt so bad that next day she died. Th' doctors thought he'd go out o' his mind an' die too. That's why he hates it. No one's never gone in since, an' he won't let any one talk about it.

Mary asked no more questions. She had much to contemplate within herself.

At that moment a very good thing was happening to her. Four good things had happened to her in fact, since she came to Misselthwaite Manor. She had felt as if she had understood a robin and that he understood her; she had run in the wind until her blood had grown warm; she had been healthily hungry for the first time in her life; and she had found out what it was to be sorry for someone.

Eventually it was her friend the robin who showed Mary where the key to the locked door was buried. He had made his home in the garden for years. When she dug it up, she looked at the key a long time.

She turned it over and over, and thought about it. . . . All she thought about the key was that if it was the key to the closed garden, and she could find out where the door was, she could perhaps open it and see what was inside the walls, and what had happened to the old rose-trees. It was because it had been shut up so long that she wanted to see it. It seemed as if it must be different from other places and that something strange must have happened to it during the ten years. Besides that, if she liked it she could go into it every day and shut the door behind her, and she could make up some play of her own and play it quite alone, because nobody would ever know where she was, but would think the door was still locked and the key buried in the earth. The thought of that pleased her very much.

Living as it were, all by herself in a house with a hundred mysteriously closed rooms and having nothing whatever to do to amuse herself, had set her inactive brain to working and was actually awakening her imagination.

Mary was beginning to care and to want to do new things. "Already she felt less 'contrary,' though she did not know why." She was enlivened by her various projects and the possibilities presenting themselves. However she was most eager to find the locked door to the walled garden which was overgrown with ivy. No matter how carefully she looked,

> she could see nothing but thickly-growing, glossy, dark green leaves. She was very much disappointed. It seemed so silly, she said to herself, to be near it and not able to get in.

She resolved to carry the key whenever she went out so she would be ready to use it if she ever did find the door.

The day after the robin led her to the key, Mary said to him, "You showed me where the key was yesterday. You ought to show me the door today." In response, he flew to the top of the wall where he sang lustily.

> What happened almost at that moment was Magic. . . . Mary had stepped close to the robin, and suddenly the gust of wind swung aside some loose ivy trails. . . . She had seen something under it. A round knob which had been covered by the leaves hanging over it. It was the knob of a door. . . . Mary's heart began to thump and her hands to shake a little in her delight and excitement. The robin kept singing and twittering away and tilting his head on one side, as if he were she. What was this under her hands which was square and made of iron and which her fingers found a hole in?
>
> It was the lock of the door which had been closed ten years and she put her hand in her pocket, drew out the key and found it fitted the keyhole. She put the key in and turned it. It took two hands to do it, but it did turn.
>
> And then she took a long breath and looked behind her up the long walk to see if any one was coming. . . . She pushed back the door which opened slowly—slowly. Then she slipped through it, and shut it behind her, and stood with her back against it, looking about her and breathing quite fast with excitement, wonder, and delight. She was standing *inside* the secret garden.

Now Mary could come through the door under the ivy any time. She felt as if she had found a world all her own.

> Everything was strange and silent and she seemed to be hundreds of miles away from any one, but somehow she did not feel lonely at all. All that

troubled her was her wish that she knew whether all the roses were dead, or if perhaps some of them had lived and might put out leaves and buds as the weather got warmer. She did not want it to be quite a dead garden. If it were a quite alive garden, how wonderful it would be, and what thousands of roses would grow on every side!

Mary called it "The Secret Garden."

She liked the name, and she liked still more the feeling that when its beautiful old walls shut her in no one knew where she was. It seemed almost like being shut out of the world in some fairy place.

The garden was completely overgrown after ten years of neglect. But Mary enthusiastically started to work in it.

She was an odd, determined little person, and now she had something interesting to be determined about, she was very much absorbed indeed. She worked and dug and pulled up weeds steadily, only becoming more pleased with her work every hour instead of tiring of it. It seemed to her like a fascinating sort of play.

Although she did not know anything about gardening, she cleared space around the "green points pushing their way through" so they might have room to breathe. Everything was so absorbing that Mary could not believe that she had been working two or three hours.

She had been actually happy all the time; and dozens and dozens of the tiny pale green points were to be seen in cleared places, looking twice as cheerful as they had looked before when the grass and weeds were smothering them.

Her intuition is accurate, but she lacks specific information about plants. She asks Martha, who says her brother Dickon knows. "Our Dickon can make a flower grow out of a brick walk. Mother says he just whispers things out o' th' ground."

It occurs to Mary that if she only had a spade and some seeds to plant, her gardening could be even better and that Dickon might be the very person to help her get these items. So with Martha's help she writes to him. He happily agrees. Mary is eager to meet him. "It was a very strange thing indeed" when she first saw him.

Figure 5. Dickon the nature boy.

She quite caught her breath as she stopped to look. . . . A boy was sitting under a tree, with his back against it, playing on a rough wooden pipe. He was a funny looking boy about twelve. He looked very clean and his nose turned up and his cheeks were as red as poppies and never had Mistress Mary seen such round and such blue eyes in any boy's face. And on the trunk of the tree he leaned against, a brown squirrel was clinging and watching him, and from behind a bush nearby a cock pheasant was delicately stretching his neck to peep out, and quite near him were two rabbits sitting up and sniffing with tremendous noses—and actually it appeared as if they were all drawing near to watch him and listen to the strange low little call his pipe seemed to make.

Clearly, Dickon lives in harmony with nature and nature responds. Recognizing his talents, Mary realizes that Dickon might be just the person who could be helpful. She asks him, "Could you keep a secret, if I told you one? It's a great secret." He assures her that he can:

I'm keepin' secrets all th' time. If I couldn't keep secrets from th'other lads, secrets about foxes' cubs, an' birds' nests, an' wild things' holes, there'd be naught safe on th' moor. Aye, I can keep secrets.

So Mary takes him into her confidence. She confesses,

I've stolen a garden. . . . It isn't mine. It isn't anybody's. Nobody wants it, nobody cares for it, nobody ever goes into it. Perhaps everything is dead in it already; I don't know.

When she shows it to him, she explains, "It's a secret garden, and I'm the only one in the world who wants it to be alive."

Dickon becomes Mary's partner in the restoration of the garden, helping her to obtain needed supplies. Also he is able to give her advice based upon his knowledge of the natural world. He assures her: "I'll come every day if tha' wants me, rain or shine. . . . It's the best fun I ever had in my life—shut in here an' wakenin' up a garden."

At the beginning of their project he reflects upon the effects of their efforts on the garden:

I wouldn't want to make it look like a gardener's garden, all clipped an' spick an' span, would you? . . . It's nicer like this with things runnin' wild, an' swinging' an catchin' hold of each other.

Mary agrees: "Don't let us make it tidy," she says. "It wouldn't seem like a secret garden if it was tidy." Gradually the garden is renewed by their care, which respects its wild aspect.

At the same time as she is spending her days cultivating the garden, Mary makes a momentous discovery at night. Periodically she has heard odd sounds emanating from a distant room in vast Misselthwaite Manor. Her inquiries about this to Martha and Mrs. Medlock were curtly dismissed. They firmly declared that these sounds were nothing, or wind from the moor, or they gave some other explanation which Mary found equally unsatisfying. One night she bravely decided to follow the sound to its source. When she came closer, she distinctly heard someone crying.

She opened the door to the room with trepidation. There she was astonished to find a young boy lying in a large four-poster bed, "crying fretfully. . . . He looked like a boy who had been ill, but he was crying more as if he were tired and cross than as if he were in pain."

After recovering from their shock, they introduce themselves. He tells her that he has to lie in bed most of the time because he is so ill that he is not expected to live. Therefore he does not want people to see him. Not even the servants are allowed to speak with him. Since he is unable to stand up, he spends his life either in bed or sitting in a chair, always isolated in his room.

This boy is Colin, son of Mr. Archibald Craven, master of Misselthwaite Manor. Colin seldom sees his father. He explains to Mary:

My mother died when I was born and it makes him wretched to look at me. He thinks I don't know, but I've heard people talking.

He tells Mary that if he lives he will become a hunchback like his father. However, he asserts, "I shan't live." Furthermore, the life he does have is confined to this one room. His father is rarely at home, and when he is he visits Colin mainly when he is asleep. Colin concludes: "He almost hates me."

Mary responds, mainly to herself: "He hates the garden, because she died." Colin asks immediately, "What garden?" Inadvertently, Mary had divulged a hint of her secret.

They talk over many things but the central image that hovers between them is the mysterious garden. Mary refers to it in vague terms, trying to conceal her involvement with it. But Colin's interest is keenly aroused:

> It was too late to be careful. He was too much like herself. He too had had nothing to think about and the idea of a hidden garden attracted him as it had attracted her. He asked question after question. Where was it? Had she never looked for the door? Had she never asked the gardeners?

He declares that he will demand to be taken there. Mary forestalls his initiative by saying,

> If the garden was a secret and we could get into it, we could watch the things grow bigger every day, and see how many roses are alive. Don't you see? Oh, don't you see how much nicer it would be if it were a secret?

Colin says he never had a secret except the one about not living to grow up. "They don't know I know that, so it is a sort of secret. But I like this kind better."

> Mary began to recover her breath and feel safer because the idea of keeping the secret seemed to please him. She felt almost sure that if she kept on talking and could make him see the garden in his mind as she had seen it he would like it so much that he could not bear to think that everybody might tramp into it when they chose.

Colin wants Mary to visit him every day, which she is eager to do. She tells him of the world she is discovering with Dickon. Colin is very interested. She confides to Martha, "I think he almost likes me." Then she asks bluntly, "Is Colin a hunchback? . . . He didn't look like one." Martha replies,

> He isn't yet. . . . But he began all wrong. . . . They was afraid his back was weak an' they've always been takin' care of it—keepin' him lyin' down and not lettin' him walk. Once they made him wear a brace but he fretted so he was downright ill. Then a big doctor came to see him an' made them take it off. He talked to th' other doctor quite rough—in a polite way. He said there'd been too much medicine and too much lettin' him have his own way.

Mary declares that she thinks Colin is a very spoiled boy. She wonders if he will die. Martha responds by giving her mother, Susan Sowerby's assessment of his situation:

> Mother says there's no reason why any child should live that gets no fresh air an' doesn't do nothin' but lie on his back an' read picture-books an' take medicine.

But he is "weak and hates th' trouble o' being taken out o' doors, an' he gets cold so easy he says it makes him ill." Mary thinks this over and wonders if it might "do him good to go out into a garden and watch things growing. It did me good."

Although Mary wanted to see Colin every day, "she did not want to see Colin as much as she wanted to see Dickon; but she wanted to see him very much." During one of her visits to Colin she mentions how different Colin is from Dickon. Of course Colin wonders who he is. She explains, "He is not like anyone else in the world. . . . He knows about everything that grows or lives on the moor." Mary believes that Dickon could give Colin some enthusiasm for life because of his love for nature. Just by speaking about Dickon the atmosphere "was all so alive that Mary talked more than she had ever talked before—and Colin both talked and listened as he had never done either before."

However it was not until much later that Mary revealed her actual discoveries to Colin. In their conversations she still was very cautious about the details of the secret garden as she and Dickon knew it. She was not confident that she could trust Colin as she trusted Dickon.

> There were certain things she wanted to find out from him, but she felt that she must find them out without asking him direct questions. In the first place, as she began to like to be with him, she wanted to discover whether he was the kind of boy you could tell a secret to. He was not in the least like Dickon, but he was evidently so pleased with the idea of a garden no one knew about that she thought perhaps he could be trusted. But she had not known him long enough to be sure.

Mary was hatching a plan. She thought to herself:

> If he could be trusted—if he really could—wouldn't it be possible to take him to the garden without having anyone find it out? The grand doctor had

said that he must have fresh air and Colin had said that he would not mind fresh air in a secret garden. Perhaps if he had a great deal of fresh air and knew Dickon and the robin and saw things growing he might not think so much about dying. When Mary had seen herself in the glass sometimes lately she realized that she looked quite a different creature from the child she had seen when she arrived from India. This child looked nice. Even Martha had seen a change in her.

Meanwhile Dickon and Mary were having a wonderful time because of their friendship and joy in the garden.

They ran from one part of the garden to another and found so many wonders that they were obliged to remind themselves that they must whisper or speak low.

Dickon also was thinking about Colin, as was Mary. They wondered if they might plan to bring him outside without anyone seeing them. Mary observes:

He knows a good many things out of books but he doesn't know anything else. He says he has been too ill to notice things and he hates going out of doors and hates gardens and gardeners. But he likes to hear about this garden because it is a secret. I daren't tell him much but he said he wanted to see it.

Before their plans progress, Mary and Colin have a huge fight which disrupts the project but nevertheless galvanizes them. That afternoon Mary preferred to spend her time with Dickon in the garden rather than visit Colin. This infuriated Colin. But Mary stood up to him.

The truth was that he had never had a fight with anyone like himself in his life and, upon the whole, it was rather good for him, though neither he nor Mary knew anything about that.

The nurse declared that it was "the best thing that could happen to the sickly pampered thing to have some one to stand up to him that's as spoiled as himself." Colin turned Mary out of the room. That was fine with her. She told him she did not want to ever come back.

Later that night Colin woke everyone with his "screaming and crying in a horrible way." Mary was frightened and angered by his "awful sounds." Her assessment was that he ought to be stopped.

> She flew along the corridor and the nearer she got to the screams the higher her temper mounted. She felt quite wicked by the time she reached the door.

She burst into his room shouting,

> You stop! . . . You stop! I hate you! Everybody hates you! I wish everybody would run out of the house and let you scream yourself to death! You *will* scream yourself to death in a minute, and I wish you would!

The shock of such an unrestrained response startled Colin so much that he actually stopped screaming and began to sob. Mary's harsh words penetrated. The "tears meant that a curious great relief had come to him." He wondered if he might live after all.

After they were reconciled, Colin said he would like to go outside with Mary and to meet Dickon, both major developments in his sequestered life. This was the moment Mary had been waiting for.

> She was so anxious that she got up from her stool and came to him and caught hold of both his hands. . . . "Can I trust you? I trusted Dickon because birds trusted him. Can I trust you—for sure—*for sure*?" she implored. Her face was so solemn that he almost whispered his answer . . . "Yes—Yes!"

She told him that Dickon would come the next day with his animals and, more than that, she had found the entrance to the secret garden. He was moved that he could enter it also, that he would live to do that. Mary told him not how she imagined the secret garden but how it really was. Colin's aches and tiredness were soon forgotten and he listened enraptured.

> That night Colin slept without once awakening and when he opened his eyes in the morning he lay still and smiled without knowing it—smiled because he felt so curiously comfortable. . . . He felt as if tight strings which had held him had loosened themselves and let him go. . . . It was so nice to have things to think about. . . . He felt that something quite new and delightful was happening to him.

The next development was that Dickon came to visit with his newborn lamb and little red fox.

> Colin slowly sat up and stared and stared—as he had stared when he first saw Mary; but this was a stare of wonder and delight. The truth was that in spite of all he had heard he had not in the least understood what this boy would be like and that his fox and his crow and his squirrels were so near to him and his friendliness that they seemed almost to be part of himself. Colin had never talked to a boy in his life and he was so overwhelmed by his own pleasure and curiosity that he did not even think of speaking. But Dickon did not feel the least shy or awkward.

He came almost daily to visit while the plans were being made as to how to transport Colin in secret to the garden. This was absorbing for all three.

> As each day passed, Colin had become more and more fixed in his feeling that the mystery surrounding the garden was one of its greatest charms. Nothing must spoil that. No one must suspect they had a secret.

Finally the afternoon arrived when Colin could be taken to the garden. Dickon pushed the wheelchair, while Mary walked beside it. "Not a human creature was to be caught sight of in the paths they took." Mary showed him all her special places as they made their way along the paths. When they reached the door to the garden he covered his face until they were inside.

> Mary and Dickon stood and stared at him. He looked so strange and different because a pink glow of colour actually crept all over him—ivory face and neck and hands and all. "I shall get well! I shall get well!" he cried out.

After this Mary and Dickon were able to bring Colin to the secret garden almost every day. He participated not only in the secret, but in the magic he found there. He was convinced that it would be in this special place, with its magical atmosphere, where he would learn to walk, a feat he does accomplish in due course. He also shares in their devoted care of the garden.

For each of the three children their belief in "the Magic" was an abiding thing. Colin also realized that "the Magic works best when you work yourself.... You can feel it in your bones and muscles." Dickon, being an animal charmer, "could see more things than most people could and many of them were things he never talked about." Mary was the animating spirit in the awakening of the garden, the revival of Colin, and the blossoming friendships. In spite of her difficult beginning in life, it seems that circumstances "were very kind to her, though she was not at all aware of it. They began to push her about for her own good."

Susan Sowerby, kindly mother of Martha and Dickon, was quietly supportive of their efforts in the garden. Near the end of the story she visits them there.

> Each of them kept looking up at her comfortable rosy face, secretly curious about the delightful feeling she gave them—a sort of warm, supported feeling. It seemed as if she understood them as Dickon understood his "creatures."

Colin tells her, "I wish you were my mother—as well as Dickon's."

> All at once Susan Sowerby bent down and drew him with her arms close against the bosom . . . as if he had been Dickon's brother. The quick mist swept over her eyes. "Eh! dear lad!" she said. "Thy own mother's in this 'ere very garden, I do believe. She couldna' keep out of it."

While the secret garden and the children were blooming together, Mr. Craven was traveling in Europe, unable to recover from his deep sorrow following the untimely death of his beloved wife Lilias. One day he felt a shift within himself.

> It was as if a sweet clear spring had begun to rise in a stagnant pool and had risen and risen until at last it swept the dark water away. . . . Something seemed to have been unbound and released in him, very quietly.

He continued his travels but,

> strange as it seemed to him, there were minutes—sometimes half-hours— when, without his knowing why, the black burden seemed to lift itself again and he knew he was a living man and not a dead one.

Summer became autumn. Then one night after a long walk, he fell into an unusually calm sleep and had a dream.

His dream was so real that he did not feel as if he were dreaming. He remembered afterward how intensely wide awake and alert he thought he was. He thought that as he sat and breathed in the scent of the late roses and listened to the lapping of the water at his feet he heard a voice calling. It was sweet and clear and happy and far away. It seemed very far, but he heard it as distinctly as if it had been at his very side.

[The voice called him by his name:] "Archie!" He thought he sprang to his feet not even startled. It was such a real voice and it seemed so natural that he should hear it. . . . [He responded:] "Lilias! Where are you?" . . . "In the garden," it came back like a sound from a golden flute. "In the garden!" And then the dream ended.

In the morning he felt changed. He pondered the dream. When the mail arrived there was a letter from Mrs. Sowerby urging him to come home. She ended it saying, "I think your lady would ask you to come if she was here." So he prepared to return to England as soon as possible.

When he arrived in Yorkshire Mr. Craven "found himself thinking of his boy as he had never thought in all the ten years past. . . . He had not meant to be a bad father, but he had not felt like a father at all." He had rarely seen his son except when he was asleep. All Mr. Craven knew of Colin was that he was a confirmed invalid, with a vicious, hysterical, half-insane temper. "He could only be kept from furies dangerous to himself by being given his own way in every detail."

But Mr. Craven's perspective was changing.

The drive across the wonderfulness of the moor was a soothing thing. Why did it seem to give him a sense of homecoming which he had been sure he could never feel again—that sense of the beauty of the land and sky and purple bloom of distance and a warming of the heart at drawing nearer to the great old house which had held those of his blood for six hundred years?

When he arrived at Misselthwaite Manor, Mr. Craven's first concern was Colin. Mrs. Medlock gave him a full report—to the best of her knowledge. She told him that Colin was presently in the garden. Mr. Craven went there immediately.

He did not walk quickly, but slowly, and his eyes were on the path. He felt as if he were being drawn back to the place he had so long forsaken, and he did not know why. As he drew near to it his step became still more slow.

As far as he knew the garden was locked and the key buried. But to his astonishment he heard children's voices inside it. Then all of a sudden, Colin came bursting through the door unexpectedly.

When Mr. Craven was led inside the garden he stood silent,

> just as the children had done when they came into its grayness. He looked round and round. . . . He said, "I thought it would be dead." . . . Colin replied, "Mary thought so at first. . . . But it came alive."

Mr. Craven is astonished by the transformation that has taken place in his son, who is now a healthy looking lad, full of enthusiasm for life. Moreover, he is able to walk. Colin explains: "It was the garden that did it—and Mary and Dickon and the creatures—and the Magic. No one knows. We kept it to tell you when you came." Mr. Craven thought it was

> the strangest thing he ever heard . . . as it was poured forth in headlong boy fashion. Mystery and Magic and wild creatures, . . . the coming of spring. . . . The odd companionship, . . . the secret so carefully kept.

Mary's ingenuity, her discovery and enthusiasm instigated the process of bringing the garden to life again. Others were drawn in. It was not a certain outcome that inspired her. Rather, having found the garden, she was interested to see what would happen when she worked in it. She wanted to learn. Life supported her efforts. Each phase had its own timing, with its own outcome, that led to the next stage. Joy came from participating in that process. At the right moment, the garden could be shared. "It need not be a secret any more."

The following chapter will explore this story as a place where the imagination can thrive, and consider some of its themes that are pertinent to the analytic process.

4

Setting and Characters in *The Secret Garden*

A story to which one feels a particular attraction is an invitation to the imagination. Dwelling in a story related to one's soul has potential for creating new insights and feelings. The imagination is the faculty that enables this to happen. The alchemists understood it to be the key that opens the door to the secret of the work. This is because the imagination responds to the symbol which participates in both the spiritual and material realms. Jung writes:

> The place or the medium of realization is neither mind nor matter, but that intermediate realm of subtle reality which can be adequately expressed only by the symbol. The symbol is neither abstract nor concrete, neither rational nor irrational, neither real nor unreal. It is always both.[73]

James Hillman relates imagination to soul:

> When the imagination is in the right place, when it is functioning correctly, it works like a mirror so that by means of it the reflection of consciousness takes place. And, though it is a mirror, imagination is an active power of the soul alone, independent of organs, and thus a purely psychic activity.[74]

Imagination liberates and renews a person with its possibilities and connections. Past, present and future are all equally valued, but also made relative as the imagination roams where it pleases. This enlivens the soul.

A Matter of Soul

What is the soul? Many of us know experientially that the soul exists and is central to our well-being. Yet, it is difficult to describe. For the apophatic writers, the soul

---

[73] *Psychology and Alchemy*, CW 12, par. 400.

[74] *Loose Ends*, p. 151.

appears to be a region of the human consciousness, its deepest level where it is aware of nothing but IS and its author—the region [Meister] Eckhart identifies as "the inner solitude." The familiar adjective "spiritual" takes on new meaning in their writings and points always in the direction of that ultimate solitude.[75]

Since there is a personal aspect to this inner solitude that is the soul, each individual may receive unique revelations about it.

Occasionally a dream will give a glimpse of the soul, which seems rather shy in essence. I sensed that the following dream gave me such a glimpse: "I suddenly saw a young woman dressed in white. She glowed in a strange way. I knew that she was one of the Shining Ones." Upon waking I made the following notation in my journal: "I feel that I have been *very* far away with this dream. It seems as if I have been in the realm of pure soul."

However, the soul has the capacity to participate in both the spiritual and physical worlds when it is embodied. It seems to desire both for its sustenance. Rabbi Adin Steinsaltz says that one of the great attributes of the soul "lies not in its abstractness, its remoteness from the physical world, but precisely in the world of living creatures, in its contact with matter."[76] Therefore it is nourished by contact with the world of the five senses, as well as by symbols which participate in the same physical and spiritual realities as the soul.

Since it is also imagined to be the eternal core of each individual, it gives a sense of participation in the divine mystery. It can infuse the activities of daily life with numinosity. It is as if the soul is the connecting link between the spirit and the body. It is inspired by spirit, but the soul in turn animates the body. Without it the body would be totally absorbed in its physiological and instinctual processes, as well as being completely vulnerable to the directives of the ego which may be quite tyrannical. The soul knows where it wants to go and what it needs if given a chance. It wants to participate in daily life, but sometimes it is so ignored as to be starving to death or so traumatized as to be imperceivable. Then there is

---

[75] Moore and Moore, eds., *The Neighborhood of IS*, pp. 13f.

[76] *The Thirteen-Petalled Rose*, p. 54.

a loss of soul, a condition so agonizingly dark as to render life a torture.

Rabbi Steinsaltz describes this life-giving phenomenon, the soul, which is somehow beyond spirit, thus immaterial, yet, in some incomprehensible way, also material. He says:

> It is beyond whatever the intellect, at its highest, can reach and understand or make clear to itself. The soul is thus not conceived as a certain defined essence, caged in the body, or even as a point of immaterial substance.[77]

Rather, it is a connecting link between the cosmos and the individual. Steinsaltz describes it as

> a continuous line of spiritual being, stretching from the source of all souls to beyond the specific body of a particular person. The connection between the body and soul is like what occurs at the end of a line of light, when a dark body is illuminated.[78]

The following dream, again one of mine, is an illustration of this connecting light between the body and soul in the darkness. The illumination was numinous both to perceive and to remember, revealing something of the reality of the soul in relation to the realms of spirit and subtle body.[79]

> It was night. I had a vantage point of a huge body of dark water which was somewhat above it, therefore I could look down and see a great distance. I could not see the boundaries of this water, where it began or where it ended. My perspective was not that complete. Or maybe there was no beginning or end to it. But I could see a lot—much more than if I were standing on the shore. It was rather as if I were in an airplane looking down—that was the view I had. But I was not in an airplane.
>
> Then I saw two luminous bodies swimming through the water. They were bright white light. Their substance was of light—not exactly, but sort of. They had form and substance, even though their essence was light. They were the only two beings I could see in the water because they were swimming very close to the surface—white light bodies moving quickly and surely through the black water.

---

[77] Ibid., pp. 54f.

[78] Ibid., p. 55.

[79] "Subtle body = the somatic unconscious, a transcendental concept involving the relationship between mind and body." (Sharp, *Jung Lexicon,* p. 129)

These two bodies seemed to belong to me. I wondered what could they be? What aspects of me are they? There was something very special about them. Then I thought, "They must be my soul and subtle body swimming together in this harmonious way in the black night sea."

The soul is a precious aspect of our being which deserves loving attention. One place where it can receive this is in a secret garden. There it can dance freely with spirit and matter.

How does the story told in *The Secret Garden* activate the imagination, an active power of the soul, in a way that mirrors consciousness? How does it mirror that which is pulsing to become conscious?

The rest of this chapter will explore answers to these questions by considering the setting and characters within the context of the story as well as on a symbolic level.

A World of One's Own

At the beginning of *The Secret Garden* the walled, locked garden had been abandoned for years, a once beautiful place in chaotic ruin. Mary was tantalized by the prospect of entering it. This human impulse to enter a forbidden area is depicted in many fairy tales. The inclination to discover what is there seems not only irresistible, but necessary for a deeper experience of life. The imagination immediately begins to supply visions of what may be found. The excitement generated fuels the next step.

When Mary, guided by the robin, unearths the key to the locked door, she is able to enter the garden for the first time. "She felt as if she had found a world all her own." This is an exhilarating moment that also stimulates the reader's imagination.

To have a world of one's own, whatever size, where one can be oneself, is to envision possibilities often not lived within the parameters of daily life. Virginia Woolf speaks of this in *A Room of One's Own*, a novel treasured by many, particularly women. Although she is talking about the oppressive features of trying to earn her own living prior to 1918, she seems to be describing the experience of many men as well as women in the present. The work was hard. It was difficult to live on the small amount of money she earned. The psychological consequences, as she sees them, are the reasons why it is so crucial for some individuals to try to find a room of their own. This is how she describes her state of mind at the time:

> I need not, I am afraid, describe in any detail the hardness of the work, for you know perhaps women who have done it; nor the difficulty of living on the money when it was earned, for you may have tried. But what still remains with me as a worse infliction than either was the poison of fear and bitterness which those days bred in me. To begin with, always to be doing work that one did not wish to do, and to do it like a slave, flattering and fawning, not always necessarily perhaps, but it seemed necessary and the stakes were too great to run risks; but then the thought of that one gift which it was death to hide—a small one but dear to the possessor—perishing and with it my self, my soul—all of this became like a rust eating away the bloom of the spring, destroying the tree at its heart.[80]

This corrosive rust that eats away "the bloom of the spring" is an agony to many in contemporary society. Having a room of one's own in a secret garden can be the place where the tree of life can be renewed at its heart. Plotinus, one of the apophatic writers, uses this image to represent a fundamental structuring principle through which the sap of life flows:

> Think of the Life coursing through some mighty tree while yet it is the stationary Principle of the whole, in no sense scattered over all that extent but, as it were, vested in the root: it is the giver of the entire and manifold life of the tree, but remains unmoved itself, not manifold but the Principle of that manifold life.[81]

The image of the tangled mess of the neglected garden is similar to the chaos one often finds when one first begins to pay attention to the unconscious and one's dreams. If the inner world has been ignored for years, it will also be confusing and difficult to recognize what may bloom and what needs pruning. It all just looks like an overgrown mess. Therefore, at the beginning of analysis one tends to start, as Mary did, by clearing some space so that the "pale green points" will have room to grow. This new life that is trying to unfold is a stimulus for the imagination. The

---

[80] *A Room of One's Own,* p. 43.

[81] Moore and Moore, eds., *The Neighborhood of IS,* p. 54.

new life grows out of the psychic soil of the unconscious like a plant.

The psyche is part of nature. But the tendency to intellectualize may block receptivity to the various dimensions of soul. Consciousness is renewed from the depths, just as a plant flourishes only when its roots grow deeply enough. It also needs sunlight and warmth in order to thrive. Similarly, though the psyche is rooted in the depths of the unconscious, the light of conscious reflection and the heat of emotion are needed to bring fruition.

Sometimes there is just too much agony and a person may be cut off from the process of renewal. Robert Johnson writes:

> We live with our psychic energy in modern times much as we do with our money—mortgaged into the next decade. Most modern people are exhausted nearly all the time and never catch up to an equilibrium of energy, let alone have a store of energy behind them. With no energy in store, one cannot meet any new opportunity.[82]

Likewise, Jung notes:

> Consciousness has strayed rather too far from the fact of the unconscious. We have even forgotten that the psyche is by no means our own design, but is for the most part autonomous and unconscious.[83]

There are many reasons for this, but healing and renewal cannot take place without the warmth of the feminine principle. The secret garden is a special setting in which to discover the manifestations of nature and to cultivate them. Eventually the right attitude can be found so that a relationship to the material arising from the depths can develop and be integrated into one's lived life.

The secret garden as a symbol which feeds the imagination and the soul has significance for both partners in the analytic process—analyst as well as analysand. It is a place where the imagination is protected, yet free. Life can be experienced differently. The ego, with its constant activity, is no longer at the center. Consciousness has its roots not in the ego and its functions (thinking, feeling, sensing and intuition) but in an-

---

[82] *The Fisher King and the Handless Maiden*, p. 93.
[83] *Psychology and Alchemy*, CW 12, par. 60.

other region of the psyche altogether, "a dimension which can only be created by the world of imagination," an inner ground that creates the life-giving symbols. "That," writes von Franz, "is why Jung calls this [inner dimension] the transcendent function."[84]

Active Imagination

In my work as an analyst I find that the secret garden as a symbol functions not only to inform the analytic process (as will be discussed at greater length in the next chapter). It is also a setting for active imagination. This is the practice of establishing a conscious dialogue with images that arise from the unconscious. Barbara Hannah writes:

> Perhaps the simplest definition of active imagination is to say that it gives us the opportunity of opening negotiations, and in time, coming to terms with these forces or figures in the unconscious.[85]

In order to do this one selects a spontaneous offering from the unconscious, such as a dream, a fantasy or a feeling, concentrates on it, then notes how it changes. One watches it carefully to see where it needs to go but does not interfere with its movement. One lets the unconscious be free to express itself.[86] "The goal is to get into touch with the unconscious, and that entails giving it an *opportunity to express itself* in some way or other."[87]

According to Marie-Louise von Franz, active imagination is particularly valuable for the practicing analyst because it can liberate one from obsessive thoughts and affects. Since an analyst is in constant contact with intense emotions and unconscious material, both of which are contagious, it is important to be clear of one session in order to be available to respond to the next analysand. It need not take more than a few minutes, but even if no time at all is available, the intent itself to deal with the situation later through active imagination can have an ameliorating effect. Von Franz considers this part of the healing work analysts must

---

[84] "The Inferior Function," in *Psychotherapy*, pp. 142f.

[85] *Encounters with the Soul: Active Imagination as Developed by C.G. Jung*, p. 16.

[86] See *Mysterium Coniunctionis*, CW 14, par. 749.

[87] Hannah, *Encounters with the Soul*, p. 17.

continually carry out on themselves. Active imagination, she writes, "is a creative act of liberation carried out through symbols."[88]

The same is true for anyone caught in intense psychic material. To engage in active imagination has some requirements, though there is no set formula. What is essential, notes von Franz, is the correct attitude.

> The proper use of active imagination can only take place in a religious context, that is, in the presence of an awe-filled, conscientious regard for the numinous.[89]

If one can enter the secret garden of the imagination and engage in this process, then it is possible to clear some psychic space for the new "green points" to emerge.

The Analytic Space as a Secret Garden

One of the practical applications of this symbol in my analytic work is that I imagine my practice room to be like a secret garden. It is a very simple room, modestly furnished. But it contains objects representing each of the four elements: earth, air, fire and water. I have created a small murmuring fountain filled with stones, shells and glass beads which I have collected over the years. It has a gentle sound of flowing water. Beside it on the floor there is a small turtle which is also a lamp that I can always see from my chair.

. This turtle lamp is not merely a decorative object. Years ago I had a dream which continues to guide me. In it I was told to go to the edge of the ocean. There, I was commanded to walk across the water.

> Horrified, I stayed on the shore pondering this strange direction. I took it seriously. It was not that I refused to go. The problem was that I did not know how to start. Then I happened to notice a dark stone in the water, at a distance that I could just reach with an extra long step. Therefore I managed that one step.
>
> As I collected my breath, I wondered, "Now what?" Then, once again, I saw another dark stone in the water onto which I could step. This happened repeatedly before I realized that each time I stepped onto a stone, it

---

[88] "Active Imagination in the Psychology of C.G. Jung," in *Psychotherapy,* p. 157.
[89] Ibid.

rose up in the water so that I had a clear place on which to stand. Finally it dawned upon me that these were not stones at all, but turtles! It seemed that there would be turtles all across the water to the far shore. So I kept walking, one step at a time. That was my path across the ocean.

This dream affected me profoundly.[90] A year later I acquired two baby turtles and two tortoises who became my beloved pets for years. They lived in the kitchen but often had adventures in the rest of our home. Whenever I entered the kitchen they became greatly excited. I felt we had a strong connection. Often they appeared in my dreams, as they do still. If they are happy I have a feeling of ecstasy. If they are suffering, I am in anguish. These animals reflected a guiding spirit in nature connected to the mysterious central fire, which was revealed in my daily contact with them, as well as in my dreams.

Figure 6. The author's pet turtles, Tully and Turtullian.

So the turtle lamp in the secret garden of my practice is a special light. It adds the element of fire to the other three elements in which the turtle

---

[90] In amplifying this dream, I came across these lines in Song of Solomon, 2:12: "Flowers appear on the earth; the time of the singing of birds is come, and the voice of the turtle is heard in our land." I did rejoice.

can function freely—earth, air and water. Thus it also represents all the elements at work in nature and therefore in the garden. The turtle is my lodestar, a guiding principle which continues to help me find my way.

Another meaningful item in the secret garden of my practice room is an almost invisible, opalescent, blown glass bulb like a tear drop. It hangs in the window. It represents an alchemical retort where the *quinta essentia* or Philosophers' Stone could be distilled. This fifth essence is all the four elements and all the four functions of consciousness, plus something more. Von Franz describes it as

> a consolidated nucleus of the personality which is no longer identical or identified with any of the functions. . . . You could call this fifth thing the urge toward individuation. When it is still unconscious, it is simply that urge toward individuation, that element of constant dissatisfaction and restlessness which nags people till they reach a higher level again and again in life.[91]

The development of this central nucleus of the personality may be assisted by work in the secret garden of analysis.

The opal bulb reminds me daily of another of my guiding dreams:

> I was desperately trying to prepare for a dinner party, but that was not the only matter on my mind. There was great confusion about trying to keep it all together, and to be ready in time. Everything was chaotic. The more I tried to prepare, the worse the whole situation became. The Dark Woman appeared. She graciously presented me with a beautiful, single red rose. At the same time she said one word to me: "Essence!"

From Jung's study of the texts written by the alchemists, he realized there were two parts to the alchemical opus: the work in the laboratory, and the theory by which it was interpreted. He writes:

> The whole process, which we understand today as psychological development, was designated the "philosophical tree," a "poetic" comparison that draws an apt analogy between the natural growth of the psyche and that of a plant.[92]

---

[91] "The Inferior Function," in *Psychotherapy,* p. 143.

[92] "The Philosophical Tree," *Alchemical Studies,* CW 13, par. 482.

Jung always emphasizes the importance of the lived experience of the psychic processes rather than a merely intellectual understanding. The latter, he says, "supplies us only with verbal concepts, but it does not give us their true content, which is to be found in the living experience of the process as applied to ourselves."[93] He notes the tragic fate of the psyche when alchemists abandoned the lived experience of the laboratory:

> Alchemy lost its vital substance when some of the alchemists abandoned the laboratorium for the oratorium, there to befuddle themselves with an ever more nebulous mysticism, while others converted the oratorium into a laboratorium and discovered chemistry. We feel sorry for the former and admire the latter, but no one asks about the fate of the psyche, which thereafter vanished from sight for several hundred years.[94]

The almost invisible opalescent bulb in my practice room keeps the image of the alchemical retort and the endeavors of the alchemists present. The essence of the analytic work is the distillation of psychological gold. The secret garden is both the laboratory where the work is done, and the library where the depths of the psyche can be acknowledged through reflection upon lived experience.

Archetypal Basis of *The Secret Garden*

An indication of the potency of *The Secret Garden* is the sense of the numinous it often generates. This connects to the archetypal material it constellates for the person in whom the story lives. The capacity for such response is important for the process of analysis, the core of which Jung considered to be an approach to the numinous. He described this in a 1945 letter:

> The main interest of my work is not concerned with the treatment of neuroses but rather with the approach to the numinous. But the fact is that the approach to the numinous is the real therapy and inasmuch as you attain to the numinous experiences, you are released from the curse of pathology. Even the very disease takes on a numinous character.[95]

---

[93] Ibid.

[94] Ibid.

[95] *C.G. Jung Letters*, vol. 1, p. 377

Von Franz comments that this passage

> says everything of essential importance about a Jungian analysis. If it is not possible to establish a relationship with the numinous, no cure is possible; the most one can hope for is an improvement in social adjustment.[96]

Figure 7. The alchemist's workplace as laboratory and library.

---

[96] "The Religious Dimension of Analysis," in *Psychotherapy,* p. 177.

The word "numinous" can be understood as an experience associated with the transcendent power of the divine. It comes from the word *numen* used by Rudolph Otto in *The Idea of the Holy*. He considers it to have both a subjective and an objective quality that inspire awe:

> There will in fact be two values to distinguish in the numen; its "fascina-tion" *(fascinans)* will be that element in it whereby it is of *subjective* value (= beatitude) to man; but it is "august" *(augustum)* in so far as it is recog-nized as possessing in itself *objective* value that claims our homage.[97]

Otto says the experience of the numinous is a "mysterium tremen-dum," because it is an encounter with the holy which is itself a tremen-dous mystery.[98] It may come to a person in many different ways, perhaps "like a gentle tide, pervading the mind with a tranquil mood of deepest worship."[99] Then it may change, passing

> into a more set and lasting attitude of the soul, continuing, as it were, thrillingly vibrant and resonant, until at last it dies away and the soul re-sumes its "profane," non-religious mood of everyday experience.[100]

It can burst from within the soul itself with sudden ecstasy or with the fluttering of its delicate butterfly wings. In whatever manner it commu-nicates itself, the effects

> become the hushed, trembling, and speechless humility of the creature in the presence of—whom or what? In the presence of that which is a *mys-tery* inexpressible and above all creatures.[101]

An experience of the numinous has important psychological effects and is central to religious experience. "There is no religion," says Otto, "in which it does not live as the real innermost core. . . . It is pre-eminently a living force in the Semitic religions."[102] Since it is a living

---

[97] *The Idea of the Holy,* p. 52.

[98] Ibid., p. 12.

[99] Ibid., pp. 12f.

[100] Ibid.

[101] Ibid.

[102] Ibid., p. 6.

force, associated with the archetypal level of the psyche, it can only be known through individual experience:

> There is only one way to help another to an understanding of it. He must be guided and led on by consideration and discussion of the matter through the ways of his own mind, until the point at which "the numinous" in him perforce begins to stir, to start into life and into consciousness. . . . [It is] awakened in the mind; as everything that comes "of the spirit" must be awakened.[103]

Numinosity is a characteristic of archetypes, the term used by Jung in reference to certain psychic phenomena. He considered an archetype to be "a living idea that constantly produces new interpretations through which that idea unfolds."[104] This "living idea" is an energy system, within the matrix of the collective unconscious, that has the capacity to constellate various motifs, patterns and symbols with a compelling, numinous quality. The word "archetype" ultimately came to cover "all psychic manifestations of a biological, psychobiological, or ideational character, provided they were more or less universal and typical."[105]

Archetypes have been compared to magnetic fields underlying the transformation of psychic processes into images. Like the word "numinous," they cannot be precisely defined. Jung explained,

> No archetype can be reduced to a simple formula. It is a vessel which we can never empty, and never fill. It has a potential existence only, and when it takes shape in matter it is no longer what it was. It persists throughout the ages and requires interpreting ever anew. The archetypes are the imperishable elements of the unconscious, but they change their shape continually.[106]

And according to Jacobi, "Every archetype is capable of infinite development and differentiation; like a robust tree it can put forth branches

---

[103] Ibid., p. 7.

[104] *Mysterium Coniunctionis,* CW 14, par. 744.

[105] Jolande Jacobi, *Complex/Archetype/Symbol in the Psychology of C.G. Jung,* p. 34.

[106] "The Psychology of the Child Archetype," *The Archetypes and the Collective Unconscious,* CW 9i, par. 301.

and thousands of magnificent blossoms."[107]

Although the origins and exact nature of archetypes are unknown and by definition unknowable, their effects can be experienced. An archetype is "a *dynamism* which makes itself felt in the numinosity and fascinating power of the archetypal image."[108] It has two aspects: one "oriented 'upward' toward the world of images and ideas, and another oriented 'downward' toward the natural biological processes—the instincts."[109]

As a symbolic expression of an archetype, the secret garden has the dynamism not only of the numinous, but also of these two aspects. One is oriented upward, toward the spiritual world. The other is oriented downward to the instinctual, biological processes. One aspect is teleological; the other indicates origin.

The Secret Garden as Symbol of the Self

The secret garden is not only a place, physical or imaginal, for feeding the soul and the imagination. It can also be understood as a symbol representing the Self, the archetype of wholeness that is the regulating center of the psyche as well as its totality. It has the elements which von Franz considers to be the basic essence of the Self: its uniting, penetrating, directive activities and its receptive, containing qualities.[110]

Since it is part of the unconscious, both personal and collective, the secret garden is not in view until the ego establishes a relationship with it. As an archetype, the Self cannot be directly perceived or represented but expresses itself through symbols in dreams, art and religion. Although eternal, the archetypes are reinterpreted through the ages. Though they are at the core of the symbols which represent them, they cannot be fully understood or explained.

We ask, along with the authors of *The Grail Legend,* "Then how and by what means can the Self become manifest?" They answer that it is

---

[107] Jacobi, *Complex/Archetype/Symbol,* p. 55.

[108] "On the Nature of the Psyche," *The Structure and Dynamics of the Psyche,* CW 8, par. 414.

[109] Jacobi, *Complex/Archetype/Symbol,* p. 39.

[110] Von Franz, *Archetypal Patterns in Fairy Tales,* p. 72.

principally in the attitude with which we approach our daily lives:

> [The Self] is realized to that extent in which it is lived in the experience of daily life. It is not achieved, however, when it appears in symbolic form in dreams and inner images, nor is it when consciousness acquires a specific degree of clarity, nor yet when a psychological function has attained a high degree of differentiation. Important as consciousness undoubtedly is—and rightly utilized consciousness is an invaluable means of help for the realization of the Self—it is not itself the determining factor. For it does not depend so very greatly on knowledge and ability or upon some degree of intelligence, but rather upon the use which is made of these attributes and above all on the psychic attitude a person adopts in the face of the various circumstances of his life and fate.[111]

The Russian novelist Boris Pasternak understood this and gave us insight into it in his great novel *Doctor Zhivago*:

> Wait, let me tell you what I think. I think that if the beast who sleeps in man could be held down by threats—any kind of threat, whether of jail or retribution after death—then the highest emblem of humanity would be the lion tamer in the circus with his whip, not the prophet who sacrificed himself. But don't you see, this is just the point—what has for centuries raised man above the beast is not the cudgel but an inward music: the irresistible power of unarmed truth, the powerful attraction of its example. It has always been assumed that the most important things in the Gospels are the ethical maxims and commandments. But for me the most important thing is that Christ speaks in parables taken from life, and He explains the truth in terms of everyday reality. The idea that underlies this is that communion between mortals is immortal, and that the whole of life is symbolic because it is meaningful.[112]

The work involved in the individuation process requires that one learn to perceive, as Pasternak says, the "inward music" and the "irresistible power of unarmed truth" in one's daily life. But it is not an automatic process. The authors of *The Grail Legend* describe its essence as follows:

---

[111] Emma Jung and Marie-Louise von Franz, *The Grail Legend*, pp. 133f.

[112] *Doctor Zhivago*, p. 42.

As the threads of fabric are woven into a pattern, so the Self as the living garment of divinity is woven out of the many decisions and crises, in themselves possibly insignificant, by which we are affected in the course of our lives. Such occasions present themselves at every level of life and intelligence and in every milieu. Whether or not they lead to a manifestation of the Self depends solely on our own response.[113]

The secret garden in our story could have been ignored forever but for the inner promptings that beckoned Mary to it. Then the transformative relationship began.

Jung considered the phenomenon of the Self to be the central point in his thinking and research.[114] In his autobiography, he recalled:

Between 1918 and 1920, I began to understand that the goal of psychic development is the self. There is no linear evolution; there is only a circumambulation of the self. Uniform development exists, at most, only at the beginning; later, everything points toward the center. This insight gave me stability, and gradually my inner peace returned. I knew that in finding the mandala as an expression of the self I had attained what was for me the ultimate. Perhaps someone else knows more, but not I.[115]

In 1927 he received confirmation of this insight in the following dream:

I found myself in a dirty, sooty city. It was night, and winter, and dark, and raining. I was in Liverpool. With a number of Swiss—say, half a dozen—I walked through the dark streets. I had the feeling that there we were coming from the harbor, and that the real city was actually up above, on the cliffs. We climbed up there. It reminded me of Basel, where the market is down below and then you climb up through the Totengässchen ("Alley of the Dead"), which leads to a plateau above and so to the Peters-platz and the Peterskirche.

When we reached the plateau, we found a broad square dimly illuminated by street lights, into which many streets converged. The various quarters of the city were arranged radially around the square. In the center was a round pool, and in the middle of it a small island. While everything

---

[113] Jung and von Franz, *The Grail Legend*, p. 134.

[114] *Memories, Dreams, Reflections*, p. 208.

[115] Ibid., pp. 196f.

round about was obscured by rain, fog, smoke, and dimly lit darkness, the little island blazed with sunlight. On it stood a single tree, a magnolia, in a shower of reddish blossoms. It was as though the tree stood in the sunlight and was at the same time the source of light.

My companions commented on the abominable weather, and obviously did not see the tree. They spoke of another Swiss who was living in Liverpool, and expressed surprise that he should have settled here. I was carried away by the beauty of the flowering tree and the sunlit island, and thought, "I know very well why he settled here." Then I awoke.[116]

Certain features of the dream represented Jung's situation at the time. "Everything was extremely unpleasant, black and opaque,"[117] just as he felt. But reflecting upon the dream he says,

I had had a vision of unearthly beauty, and that was why I was able to live at all. Liverpool is the "pool of life." The "liver," according to an old view, is the seat of life—that which "makes to live."[118]

He interprets this as a revelation about the Self:

This dream brought with it a sense of finality. I saw that here the goal had been revealed. One could not go beyond the center. The center is the goal, and everything is directed toward that center. Through this dream I understood that the self is the principle and archetype of orientation and meaning. Therein lies its healing function.[119]

The story of the secret garden embodies this principle and archetype of orientation, the Self, to which Jung refers. The children experienced the healing numinosity that radiated to them through the garden.

When Mary and Dickon were there together they found "every joy on earth." When Colin first gazed upon the garden it had such an uplifting effect upon him that he declared, "I shall get well! And I shall live forever!" Because of the secret garden Mary started to like being outside. "She no longer hated the wind, but enjoyed it." She forgot her shyness

---

[116] Ibid., pp. 197f.
[117] Ibid., p. 198.
[118] Ibid., p. 197.
[119] Ibid., pp. 198f.

and began to make friends. Her taciturn, disagreeable disposition softened into a spunky spiritedness.

Colin was convinced that through daily contact with the garden he would be healed. His intuition proved to be accurate. Eventually, after he had been taken to the garden as planned, his doctor remarked, "The boy is a new creature." "So is the girl," said Mrs. Medlock:

> She's begun to be downright pretty since she's filled out and lost her ugly little sour look. The glummest, ill-natured little thing she used to be and now her and Master Colin laugh together like a pair of crazy young ones.

Another characteristic feature of the Self that was experienced in the garden was what the children called "Magic." Colin sensed, *"Something is there—something!"*

> "It's Magic," said Mary. . . . They always called it Magic and indeed it seemed like it in the months that followed—the wonderful months—the radiant months—the amazing ones.

Colin describes what happened:

> When Mary found this garden it looked quite dead. . . . Then something began pushing things up out of the soil and making things out of nothing. . . . I keep saying to myself, "What is it? What is it? It's something. It can't be nothing! I don't know its name so I call it Magic. . . . Magic is always pushing and drawing and making things out of nothing.

There is something of ultimate value, a soul quality, about the garden. When Mary entered it for the first time, she realized,

> It was different from any other place she had ever seen in her life. "How still it is!" she whispered. "How still!" Then she waited a moment and listened at the stillness.

Compare this to Meister Eckhart's remark:

> In the essence of the soul [is] the central silence . . . . where no creature may enter, nor any idea, . . . either of itself or of anything else.
>   I like best those things in which I see most clearly the likeness of God. Nothing in all creation is so like God as stillness.[120]

---

[120] Moore and Moore, eds., *The Neighborhood of IS,* p. 47.

The broad setting for the story and the garden is the moor, which can be viewed as a metaphor for the unconscious. On her first encounter with it, "Mary felt as if the drive would never come to an end and that the wide bleak moor was a wide strip of black ocean through which she was passing on a strip of dry land." But soon she meets Martha who has a completely different feeling about it. She sees its beauty. She tells Mary,

> I just love it. . . . It's covered wi' growin' things as smells sweet. It's fair lovely in spring an' summer when th' gorse an' broom an' heather's in flower. It smells o' honey an' there's such a lot o' fresh air—an' th' sky looks so high an' th' bees an' skylarks make such a nice noise hummin' an' singin'. Eh! I wouldn't live away from the moor for anything.

The moor has many moods. It can be stormy, generating a "wutherin' wind so strong that one could barely stand up in it." After a storm it has a different aspect. "The far-reaching world of the moor itself looked softly blue instead of gloomy purple-black or awful dreary gray." It was a gentle gust of moor wind that blew aside the ivy covering the walls of the garden long enough for Mary to spot the door knob which had been hidden. This enabled her to gain entrance to the secret garden. Dickon appreciates the good rich moor earth. He observes:

> It's in good humor makin' ready to grow things. It's glad when plantin' time comes. It's dull in th' winter when it's got nowt to do. In th' flower gardens out there things will be stirrin' down below in th' dark.

The moor has the same quality of Magic as the secret garden. One morning Mary looked out the window to see that the moor was blue "and the whole world looked as if something Magic had happened to it." Similarly, the unconscious can seem barren, or even not to exist when one considers it at first. But then, sometimes with the help of someone who has a loving connection with it, one can see its beauty, variety and richness, as well as respect its unpredictability, even storminess.

The Psychological Situation

It is not only the setting of the story that engages the imagination and touches the soul. It is also the characters. Each suggests various levels of meaning. Both Mary and Colin are abandoned, lonely children. They embody the characteristics of the child archetype. According to Jung, one of the principle features of this is in fact abandonment.

> Abandonment, exposure, danger, etc. are all elaborations of the "child's" insignificant beginnings and of its mysterious and miraculous birth. This statement describes a certain psychic experience of a creative nature, whose object is the emergence of a new and as yet unknown content.[121]

Although this is an agonizing situation, it has the potential to bring new life to the personality, as can be seen in the story.

Another quality of this archetype is the invincibility of the child:

> It is a personification of vital forces quite outside the limited range of our conscious mind; of ways and possibilities of which our one-sided conscious mind knows nothing; a wholeness which embraces the very depths of Nature. It represents the strongest, the most ineluctable urge in every being, namely the urge to realize itself.[122]

Certainly there is great satisfaction in seeing Mary struggle through her adversities to find new life, not only for herself but also for Colin. He is part of this archetypal picture because a third characteristic of the child archetype is that it has both a feminine and a masculine nature.[123] Finally, it is both beginning and end. "Psychologically speaking, this means that the 'child' symbolizes the pre-conscious and the post-conscious essence of man."[124]

Mary was orphaned when her parents died of cholera. Colin became an orphan psychologically when his mother died shortly after his birth and his father withdrew from life because of grief. Mary had always been kept "out of the way," even when her parents were alive. She had been attended by servants who did everything for her. By the time she was orphaned at ten years of age, she was a tyrannical, selfish, disagreeable girl unable to do anything for herself.

---

[121] "The Psychology of the Child Archetype," *The Archetypes and the Collective Unconscious,* CW 9i, par. 285.

[122] Ibid., par. 289.

[123] Ibid., par. 292.

[124] Ibid., par. 299.

She was delivered into the custody of her uncle, Mr. Craven, whose deputy, the housekeeper Mrs. Medlock, had the responsibility of managing life at Misselthwaite Manor, serving Mr. Craven unquestioningly. But he had lost his Eros when his wife died. He traveled like a ghost in the underworld. There was no animating spirit in the household. There were only rules enforced by Mrs. Medlock in an effort to please Mr. Craven (an impossible task) and to maintain her position.

Meanwhile, Mr. Craven's son, Colin, the young heir and possibility for the next generation, languished in his room expecting to die. He could not enter life. The door was locked and the key lost, just as it was for Mary. Rejected by his father and isolated, he was unable to either stand on his own or walk. He was as tyrannical as Mary. The situation was dismal.

If this is imagined as representing a psychological condition, the problem is that the animating spirit or principle of life is missing. Also, in terms of analytical psychology, it could be said that Mary lacks contact with her inner masculine (the animus) which would enable her to have a meaningful relationship with the world around her and to have some capacity to take care of herself (for example, to dress herself). She has no standpoint in life because she is so isolated. Her energy has no outlet, therefore it turns nasty. However, she has a healthy instinct that eventually leads her to connect with her wounded masculine side.

Similarly, Colin lacked a relationship with his inner feminine (the anima) which would enable him to find his standpoint and enjoy life. As an aspect of Mary's young, wounded animus, Colin first needs to learn to walk. Neither child has experienced good mothering. Therefore they are isolated, cut off from a vital engagement with life.

There is in each of us an innate psychological need to be in contact with a positive, nurturing feminine approach. In our story, in the absence of the personal mother, this came from nature, as well as the warmth of Martha and her mother Mrs. Sowerby. Indeed, Dickon too had a well-developed feminine side, which could not be said of the housekeeper, Mrs. Medlock, who was governed by rules and fear.

Misselthwaite Manor had been lacking the animating spirit of Eros for ten years. Everyone suffered because of its absence. "In Plato's writings, Eros is . . . considered the source of fertility and an inspiring force in all spiritual achievements."[125] Jung quotes a description of Eros as a "mighty daemon" that is "not the whole of our inward nature, though he is at least one of its essential aspects."[126]

Eros functions as a connecting principle and source of creativity. It is the feeling of vitality, meaning and desire for life, the capacity for devotion to one's own processes, as well as to others. It enhances the ability to search for the right relationship to living. Von Franz: "A person who meets someone in whom Eros is alive feels the mysterious inner nucleus behind his humble human ego, for he has creativity, life, and vitality."[127]

Clearly, then, the lack of Eros at the beginning of our story depicts a miserable, even devastating, situation of psychological stasis and spiritual impoverishment, a living death in the midst of material wealth.

How is life to flow again? It has to be renewed from its source. In the story this is the moor and the garden, or, understood psychologically, the archetypal world of the unconscious. Out of the nadir of loneliness found at the beginning, something new is constellated. This may not always happen, but it is an uplifting feature of *The Secret Garden*. Indeed, Jung does not view loneliness negatively, even though one may experience it as such. He says that a person

> must be alone if he is to find out what it is that supports him when he can no longer support himself. Only this experience can give him an indestructible foundation.[128]

When Mary becomes aware of her helplessness and feelings of loneliness, she has found the first seeds of her awakening. This happens in her relationship to Martha, the young Yorkshire girl assigned to be Mary's maid. Martha explains that if there had been "a grand Missus at Mis-

---

[125] Marie-Louise von Franz, *The Golden Ass of Apuleius: The Liberation of the Feminine in Men,* p. 82.

[126] *Two Essays,* CW 7, pars. 32f.

[127] Von Franz, *Golden Ass,* p. 97.

[128] *Psychology and Alchemy,* CW 12, par. 32.

selthwaite," she would never have been allowed to accept a position other than as scullery maid. She understands the reason for this. "I'm too common an' talk too much Yorkshire." But her love of life, her spontaneous reactions uninhibited by a constricting sense of etiquette, are qualities that are crucial for Mary's development.

Martha has values different from any Mary has encountered before. She is one of twelve children in a poor but loving family. She has a natural understanding about life. She expresses her feelings and reactions frankly. She sees Mary realistically and does not hesitate to tell her what she sees. So Mary is reflected, mirrored, by someone for the first time. From Martha she learns that children are expected to learn to dress themselves so they do not have to be waited on hand and foot. She also learns about family life and Dickon who will soon become her friend. It is from Martha that she first hears about the locked garden. Martha urges her to go outside, to start exploring, to learn to play and not just sit in her room all day doing nothing.

Martha represents a spontaneous feminine spirit, not circumscribed by rules. Her world is imbued with love for both nature and people. She has clarity about what is needed. She also has the ability to act according to her perceptions. Mary needs contact with this approach to life. But the only reason Martha and Mary are able to have a relationship is because of the problem presented at the beginning of the story: there is no capable feminine principle, no "grand missus," no Eros. Therefore Martha, who embodies a healing approach to life, is able to slip into the establishment through the back door, as it were.

In the Biblical story, Martha also functions as a servant, although Mary is her sister. When Jesus came to visit, Mary sat at his feet listening to him speak. Meanwhile, Martha was busy serving. She came to Jesus and said,

> Lord, dost thou not care that my sister hath left me to serve alone? bid her therefore that she help me. And Jesus answered and said unto her, Martha, Martha, thou art careful and troubled about many things: But one thing is needful: and Mary hath chosen that good part, which shall not be taken away from her. (Luke 10:40-42; Authorized King James Version)

This can be seen as an account of the tension that arises within a person dedicated to duty, when confronted with someone nearby appreciating life in the neighborhood of being, or IS. Intrapsychically it can be interpreted as the conflict of these two parts within one personality. While a part of the person listens to the divine teaching, the stirring of the soul, another, immersed in practicalities, has no peace. However, Martha of *The Secret Garden*, in her spontaneous way, seems to encompass both being and doing, whereas Mary was ill prepared for either at the beginning of the story.

Following Martha's direction, Mary ventures outside to explore. As she was trying to find her bearings,

> she saw a bird with a bright red breast . . . and suddenly he burst into his winter song—almost as if he had caught sight of her and was calling to her. She stopped and listened to him and somehow his cheerful, friendly little whistle gave her a pleased feeling—even a disagreeable little girl may be lonely, and the big closed house and the big bare moor and big bare gardens had made this one feel as if there was no one left in the world but herself. If she had been an affectionate child, who had been used to being loved it would have broken her heart, but even though she was "Mistress Mary Quite Contrary" she was desolate, and the bright-breasted little bird brought a look into her sour little face which was almost a smile. She listened to him until he flew away.

Mary's spirit quickens with the robin and Ben Weatherstaff in nature, outside the massive, gloomy manor. Psychologically, it is not the ego that finds the solution to the situation. Rather, the ego in response to the bird opens to the unexpected, delicate revelations of the present moment. Symbolically, the robin can be regarded as a form of intuition and spirit in harmony with nature. Ben Weatherstaff, the old gardener, is faithful to the gardens, as was Mrs. McIntyre (described in chapter two). His masculine knowledge about how to support the natural processes is part of the structure the children need for their own explorations.

The key that opens the possibility of a relationship between Ben and Mary is, again, not the ego but the realization that they share a mutual experience of loneliness. Psychologically this would be a relationship that supports the gaining of transformative knowledge, not mere facts.

Ben Weatherstaff is a masculine consciousness in the service of Mother Nature. He knows about her cyclical rhythms and her gradual, spiral pattern of growth. When Mary also becomes related to these processes she is able to connect with her masculine side, her animus.

Dickon, Martha's young brother, is twelve years old. He is the only child in the story to have a loving mother, Susan Sowerby. Martha tells Mary that Dickon is "a kind lad an' animals like him." One of his animal friends is a pony he found on the moors. "It got to like him so it follows him about an' lets him get on its back."

> Mary had never possessed an animal pet of her own and had always thought she should like one. So she began to feel a slight interest in Dickon, and as she had never before been interested in anyone but herself, it was the dawning of a healthy sentiment.

Mary imagines Dickon out on the moors by himself playing with his animals. This inspires her, so that when Martha suggests she also go out by herself, the ground has been prepared. She starts her own explorations of the world outside.

Like Ben Weatherstaff, Dickon loves nature. When Mary first sees him, he is leaning against a tree, playing a wooden pipe with his animal friends—a squirrel, a bird and rabbits—enjoying the concert. When he slowly gets up to talk with her, he explains, "A body 'as to move gentle an' speak low when wild things is about." He is a Pan figure, a young "green man" connected to the physical, natural earth.[129] Mary wondered "if it was possible for him to quietly turn green and put out branches and leaves." Nature is Dickon's life, his joy. He has Eros for everything in it. He is well connected to the moor, the plants and the animals. He says that what is needed for the animals to thrive is to be friends with them, but he also knows that "a body had better not meddle."

Dickon represents a healthy connection with the instinctive, animal side of life. In fairy tales, if the hero or heroine has a good relationship with the animals, matters usually turn out well in the end. Animals fol-

---

[129] See Graham Jackson, *The Secret Lore of Gardening: Patterns of Male Intimacy*, p. 12.

low their own inner order of what they are meant to be (e.g., tigers don't long to be elephants), knowing exactly the right timing. Connecting with this capacity is imperative if one is not to be constantly violating one's own nature. Both Mary and Colin needed to find some grounding in the instinctive side of life.

Dickon's capacity for Eros is also apparent in his relationships with Mary and Colin. He meets Mary's enthusiasm for the garden with sensitivity. Without his help, she could not have made any progress, even though her imagination was on fire. She needed his practical knowledge, his youthful, masculine strength as well as the harmony with which he moved in the world. Dickon produces the seeds Mary wants for the garden. They work together every day, preparing the ground and planting.

> The seeds grew as if fairies had tended them. Satiny poppies of all tints danced in the breeze by the score, gaily defying flowers which had lived in the garden for years and which it might be confessed seemed rather to wonder how such new people got there. And the roses—the roses! Rising out of the grass, tangled round the sun-dial, wreathing the three trunks and hanging from their branches, climbing up the walls and spreading over them with long garlands falling in cascades—they came alive day by day, hour by hour. Fair fresh leaves, and buds—tiny at first but swelling and working Magic until they burst and uncurled into cups of scent delicately spilling themselves over their brims and filling the garden air.

Again, they always felt that they were participating in an exhilarating mystery which they called Magic.

Mary blossomed in relationship to Dickon and the garden, leaving behind her imperious crankiness. Colin was also affected by Dickon's Eros. When they went to the garden every day, "it was Dickon who showed him the best things of all." Dickon understood what Colin felt better than Colin did himself. "He understood by a sort of instinct so natural that he did not know it was understanding."

Although there is no mother present at the beginning of the story, she soon emerges. It becomes apparent that Susan Sowerby, mother of twelve including Martha and Dickon, has room in her heart for Mary and Colin also. As the story progresses, her kindly presence in the background is quietly supportive to all. Colin observes, "Magic is in her just as it is in Dickon. . . . It makes her think of ways to do things. She is a Magic person." He tells her, "You are just what I wanted . . . I wish you were my Mother as well as Dickon's."

At the end of the book, his own mother, Lilias Craven, appears to her husband, Archie. When Archie asks, "Lilias! Where are you?" she replies, "In the garden!" There is a feeling that her soul has been in the garden all along, imparting her love to the children.

Ending or Need for a New Beginning?

By working and playing together in the garden the children are changed. Eventually they become strong enough to share their secret. The vitality they found radiated to others, affecting the whole situation at Misselthwaite Manor. The animating feminine spirit that was missing at the beginning of the story is present again.

Ironically the first "green points" in its recovery came from Mary's adversities. "Circumstances . . . were very kind to her, though she was not at all aware of it. They began to push her about for her own good." Her response to these circumstances that were pushing her about led to the various relationships that fostered new life. However, at the end of the story Mary seems to disappear. Colin and his father walk across the lawn together causing much astonishment and rejoicing among all at Misselthwaite Manor. But where is Mary?

It is as if the story has given a hint of a solution to the psychological problem, but it is not fully established. The masculine father and son reunion does not seem to have room for Mary. It reminds me of my dream of the Dark Woman locked up in a cage at the back of the house exclaiming, "It's my party!" Will the new order at Misselthwaite Manor suffer again from the loss of the animating feminine spirit represented by Mary? Perhaps the work and pleasure in the garden will continue another day. But that is for the imagination to supply. The story does not.

Since *The Secret Garden* was written early in the twentieth century, it is interesting to imagine what it may reveal about the psychic conditions prevailing in Western culture at the time. When the ending of the story is considered symbolically, there are disturbing indications about the de-

veloping orientation for the rest of the century. In view of these reflections, the healing quality inherent in the symbol of the garden will be
even more apparent.

In the following discussion the terms masculine and feminine are used
to refer to qualities present in the psychology of both men and women as
well as in the cosmos. This corresponds to Jung's use of the terms in his
commentary on "The Secret of the Golden Flower." It is a Taoist conception that masculine implies the *yang* principle. Its quality is to rise
upward and expand. The feminine principle is *yin* which moves downward, is connected to the earth and the bodily soul. These qualities are
associated with the psychic processes of Logos and Eros, respectively.
Jung distinguishes between the two as follows:

> Eros is an interweaving; Logos is differentiating knowledge, clarifying
> light. Eros is relatedness, Logos is discrimination and detachment.[130]

Since the feminine principle is more connected to the earth, it also
manifests as the relatedness of Eros. In contrast, the masculine principle,
associated with rising into the air, has an affinity with the sword of dis-
crimination and detachment that are connected to Logos.

If *The Secret Garden* is considered as a metaphor for the cultural
situation at the beginning of the twentieth century, it could be said that
the patriarchal world had lost its Eros, its animating connection with the
world. The effects of the Industrial Revolution were being felt, but the
Edwardian period still had vestiges of the earlier life. As the century
closed, however, it was clear that the culture had been deeply affected by
this loss of Eros. For many people the major portion of each day was
spent functioning anonymously in utilitarian, goal-directed activities
which were not valued in themselves.

At the beginning of the story the main relationship with the feminine
side of life is between servant and master. The feminine principle in the
form of Mrs. Medlock serves the master whom she fears. The feminine
principle is also present in Mary who initially has no standpoint. The
situation is bleak but not hopeless, because of Martha and her mother,

---

[130] *Alchemical Studies,* CW 13, par. 60.

Mrs. Sowerby. Though poverty stricken and socially marginal, they are well grounded in the feminine side of life. They radiate this to others. The masculine energy—personified by Colin—which is meant to inherit the world of privilege, is isolated, also without a standpoint from which to function. It is tyrannical in character. At the same time, the young feminine principle has been abandoned. Forsaken, this energy is also tyrannical. The Eros quality that the patriarchal world lost at the beginning of the story cannot be transmitted to the next generation.

As the twentieth century progressed, Western industrialized society developed a rational, secular ideology of productivity, with speed and consumerism being the normative orientation to success. More recently the computer has also had a determining influence. Combining speed and productivity, as well as facilitating a certain type of growth, it has become almost a cultural icon. It has also added another feature to collective values: the "program." If one has the right program and knows how to use it, the goal is assured. This one-sided emphasis is potentially pathological. Power rules without respect for the natural rhythms inherent in the earthy, feminine energy of Eros.

Without an animating Eros connection to the ebb and flow of life, the new generation, the new psychological development, is stuck. Lacking relatedness, psychic energy spins in its own orbit, always inside the same loop. Then it becomes increasingly tyrannical, demanding to be served. The compulsive drive for more, more, more, which is a form of possession, crushes the spark of life. Central to this is a great vortex of emptiness, like a black hole. The emphasis in the culture upon constant growth and the accumulation of material goods is a form of greed which is itself a tyrant. It creates a radical detachment from the instinctual level of the psyche and therefore from the central fire of life.

Jung identified this problem in Western culture. In *The Undiscovered Self* he formulates it as an inherent dissociation between the intellect and the instincts:

> Nothing estranges man more from the ground plan of his instincts than his learning capacity, which turns out to be a genuine drive toward progressive transformations of human modes of behaviour. It, more than anything

else, is responsible for the altered conditions of our existence and the need for new adaptations which civilization brings.[131]

He also points out how the conflict created by this cultural separation of intellect from instinct affects individual lives:

> Separation from his instinctual nature inevitably plunges civilized man into the conflict between conscious and unconscious, spirit and nature, knowledge and faith, a split that becomes pathological the moment his consciousness is no longer able to neglect or suppress his instinctual side.[132]

Jung says that the nature of this pathological situation is the result of our increasing alienation from the instinctual foundations of living, combined with aligning ourselves with conscious knowledge and degrading the unconscious. Most of our energy is spent investigating the world around us and adapting to it.

> This task is so exacting and its fulfilment so advantageous, that he forgets himself in the process, losing sight of his instinctual nature and putting his own conception of himself in place of his real being.[133]

The mechanism of dissociation can occur when psychic material such as fantasies gain enough energy to start to break into consciousness. When these are too unacceptable to the status quo of ego consciousness, a conflict will develop which is often difficult to bear, so the personality may split into different characters in an effort to cope. This does not usually happen suddenly. Such dissociation, notes Jung,

> had been prepared long before in the unconscious, when the energy flowing off from consciousness (because unused) strengthened the negative qualities of the unconscious personality, and particularly its infantile traits.[134]

This seems to be the root condition of many individuals in analysis:

---

[131] *The Undiscovered Self,* p. 92.

[132] Ibid., p. 93.

[133] Ibid.

[134] Ibid., p. 80.

each, in different ways, has lost sight of his or her instinctual nature and has established a conception of themselves in place of their real being. (Of course, this is also true of many not in analysis.) There has been a radical forgetting or rejection of the inner self, tyrannical control of the instinctual aspects of life, a fierce attempt to live an ideal image of oneself. Whatever does not serve the aims of the ego is banished and finally dissociated from the person's conscious life. But these split-off elements of the psyche—to which Jung gave the name complexes, now a household word—remain alive in the unconscious, pulsing with their own energy. Eventually they begin to attract attention to themselves by causing symptoms such as anxiety or depression or some other illness, physical or psychological.

The dissociated elements, or complexes, form what can be thought of as subpersonalities that may contain valuable qualities with which the ego has no contact because they do not conform to one's conscious self-concept. The ego tries its best to maintain control of these various elements. Jung compares this situation to a crowd being controlled by a dictator:

> Just as the chaotic movements of the crowd, all ending in mutual frustration, are impelled in a definite direction by a dictatorial will, so the individual in his dissociated state needs a directing and ordering principle. Ego-consciousness . . . overlooks the existence of powerful factors which thwart its intentions.[135]

On the one hand the ego exerts control to the best of its ability, and on the other, there are forces at work in the unconscious that may begin to tear a person apart. For some people, the dissociation eventually becomes a source of agony. A one-sided attitude can no longer be maintained because the cost is too great. Efforts to ignore the inner reality become increasingly fruitless, or worse, deleterious.

Jung says that what is urgently needed in such a situation is a form of order and synthesis. But how is this to occur when a person has spent a lifetime without any appreciation of the dynamics of the inner world and

---

[135] Ibid., pp. 73f.

has always understood order to mean control? Jung's answer is that if a person wants to reach the goal of synthesis, one must first get to know the nature of the factors at work within. The ego "must *experience* them, or else it must possess a numinous *symbol* that expresses them and conduces to synthesis."[136] Elsewhere, Jung describes symbols as "the best possible expressions for something unknown—bridges thrown out towards an unseen shore."[137]

The secret garden is just such a symbol functioning as a bridge to a far shore. In our story it activated the alchemy of Mary's imagination. Everyone who became involved with her contributed to the garden's renewal. Proceeding step by step as the way opened, they participated in its "Magic" and were changed. It was not only the garden that woke up.

Similarly, today, the secret garden, notionally or concretely, provides a temenos wherein the banished, dissociated fragments of the psyche may gradually be recovered. This is not a collective program. It is a uniquely individual path of discovery and relationship.

The next chapter explores some aspects of this process in the temenos of the secret garden. Perhaps it is the fruition of some of the seeds sown by the ingenious Mary. Even though she seems to disappear at the end of the story, her feisty resourcefulness inspires an impression that she will find her path, however obscure it may seem.

Mary's discovery of the secret garden was a gift which has activated the imagination of generations of readers. Entering it in order to find one's own living connection with the animating spirit of Eros that has vanished from view constitutes a new beginning.

---

[136] Ibid., p. 74.

[137] "On the Relation of Analytical Psychology to Poetry," *The Spirit in Man, Art, and Literature,* CW 15, par. 116.

5
Gardens, Secrets and Individuation

At the beginning of our story, the garden was inaccessible, abandoned, desolate and chaotic. It contained both life and death, joy and despair. It had been a sanctuary for Lilias and Archie Craven, separate from their usual world, functioning as a temenos, a sacred place. Later it functioned in a similar way for the children. To her delight, Mary realized that it was "not quite a dead garden." It became a place of exploration, discovery, play, privacy, friendship, work, magic, healing and celebration.

By the end of the story the garden was transformed, as were Mary and Colin. Working and playing within its walls were remedies for their wounds, while the garden contained their energy, imagination and excitement. The children tilled the earth, planted the seeds, gave the garden their love. In the temenos of the garden they became aware that, in the language of Eastern philosophy,

> the secret of the magic of life consists in using action in order to attain non-action. One must not leap over everything and penetrate directly.[138]

For most of the story the garden had to be a closely guarded secret. The discoveries and activities of Mary and Colin had to be protected from interference by others. Moreover their own energy needed protection from streaming outward, thereby exhausting itself. In the sacred precinct of a temenos the innermost personality is protected by preventing the flowing out of psychic energy and is guarded from external influences.[139] The worlds of being and becoming can mingle safely here. The secret also gave them energy. Jung explains:

> It is important to have a secret, a premonition of things unknown. It fills life with something impersonal, a *numinosum*. A man who has never experienced that has missed something important. He must sense that he lives

---

[138] Richard Wilhelm, *The Secret of the Golden Flower: A Chinese Book of Life,* p. 21
[139] Ibid., par. 36.

in a world which in some respects is mysterious; that things happen and can be experienced which remain inexplicable; that not everything which happens can be anticipated. The unexpected and the incredible belong in this world. Only then is life whole.[140]

Similarly, in the imagination a secret is potent. Jung writes:

Like the initiate of a secret society who has broken free from the undifferentiated collectivity, the individual on his lonely path needs a secret which for various reasons he may not or cannot reveal. Such a secret reinforces him in the isolation of his individual aims. A great many individuals cannot bear this isolation.[141]

But isolation can be a stimulus to the psyche. Elsewhere Jung explains:

Isolation by a secret results as a rule in an animation of the psychic atmosphere, as a substitute for loss of contact with other people. It causes an activation of the unconscious. . . . The mechanism of these phenomena can best be explained in terms of energy. Our normal relations to objects in the world at large are maintained by a certain expenditure of energy. If the relation to the object is cut off there is a "retention" of energy, which creates an equivalent substitute.[142]

As a child of about ten, Jung himself had a secret. He had experienced himself as splitting, turning into a prankish boy he neither liked nor recognized. He feared this, sensing that his inner security was threatened. He says, "My disunion with myself and uncertainty in the world at large led me to an action which at the time was quite incomprehensible to me."[143] He carved a little figure, put it in a box with an oblong stone which he painted, hid in the attic, and visited periodically.

All this was a great secret. . . . No one could discover my secret and destroy it. I felt safe, and the tormenting sense of being at odds with myself was gone.[144]

---

[140] *Memories, Dreams, Reflections,* p. 356.

[141] Ibid., p. 343.

[142] *Psychology and Alchemy,* CW 12, par. 57.

[143] *Memories, Dreams, Reflections,* p. 21.

[144] Ibid.

He did not try to explain this.

> [I] was satisfied to possess something that no one knew and no one could
> get at. . . . an inviolable secret which must never be betrayed, for the safety
> of my life depended on it. Why that was so I did not ask myself. It simply
> was so.[145]

Jung realized that the possession of a secret had a powerful effect on
his character. In fact, he considered it to be the essential factor in his
childhood. Reflecting late in life, he wrote:

> There is no better means of intensifying the treasured feeling of individu-
> ality than the possession of a secret which the individual is pledged to
> guard.[146]

Thirty years later Jung recalled his secret world. In contrast, his life in
Zurich seemed alien to him, from "some remote world and time,"[147]
compared to the period of his childhood in which he had become absorbed in his secrets. He considered that to be eternal. He writes, "I have
never forgotten that moment, for it illuminated in a flash of lightning the
quality of eternity in my childhood."[148]

In *The Secret Garden,* Mary knew that she could trust Dickon and
Colin only if they could keep a secret. The energy generated had a vivi-
fying effect. It was made more precious by the fellowship of the three
soul-mates who shared the secret. One reason why the story is so ap-
pealing, even uplifting, is because the children protect their secret but
they are not entirely isolated by it. They have each other. Jung notes that
on an individual level,

> the experience of the unconscious is a personal secret communicable only
> to very few, and that with difficulty; hence the isolating effect . . . . But
> isolation brings about a compensatory animation of the psychic atmos-
> phere which strikes us as uncanny.[149]

---

145 Ibid., p. 22.

146 Ibid., p. 342.

147 Ibid., p. 20.

148 Ibid., pp. 20f.

149 *Psychology and Alchemy,* CW 12, par. 61.

This "animation of the psychic atmosphere" can be fruitful in the private yet shared reality of the analytic relationship, which can reduce the isolation while still maintaining the secret.

In our story, when the work in the garden was firmly established, the garden could be opened. It no longer had to be a secret. From the nurturing the children had both given and received within it, they became strong enough to participate in a larger world. Life began to break in.

Similarly, in the course of analysis one eventually has to take out into life what one has gained. There may be struggles. But there is sustenance in the knowledge of the secret garden of the soul. This brings an added dimension to life: one may be alone, but not lonely, when the inner garden is being cultivated.

Inside the temenos of the secret garden the children were not only protected, they were also inspired by a sense of purpose. It was a sacred place which gave their lives meaning and changed them. Within its walls a new world was revealed, different from the pain of isolation, loneliness and lameness. There was a break in their habitual perceptions. Eventually they developed a changed orientation to life because of their discoveries in this temenos, this safe, sacred place.

In an experience of the sacred there is separation from ordinary life and an opening to a transcendent reality emanating from the eternal realm; it touches the soul, thereby centering life. Sacred time is circular and renewing because of the experience of something felt to be eternal. In contrast, a completely secular attitude to life is homogenous, linear, historical (beginning with birth, ending with death). Repetition without the sacred brings boredom, even pessimism, because it has no meaning beyond personal events.

A life devoid of the sacred is concretized; it transmits no message of meaning because there is no sense of life beyond the known human condition. In a world devoid of the sacred, there is generally much activity but little renewal. Eventually one may yearn for something more. But what is it? If this "more" is on the same level as what has gone before, there is little satisfaction, whereas in contact with the sacred the soul is nourished.

Robert Johnson calls this "a feeling that goes to the very heart of life . . . . the feeling of reverence."[150]

The temenos of the secret garden can also be seen as a mandala, which is not only a means of expression but has a demonstrable effect. A mandala is an enclosing circle or square which is a manifestation of two sources: the unconscious nature and an intuition of the Self. Jung says that it protects a person "from the 'perils of the soul' that threaten him from without and attack anyone who is isolated by a secret."[151] In his autobiography he writes:

> When I began drawing mandalas . . . I saw that everything, all the paths I had been following, all the steps I had taken, were leading back to a single point—namely, to the mid-point. [See Figure 8, page 96.] It became increasingly plain to me that the mandala is the center. It is the exponent of all paths. It is the path to the center, to individuation.[152]

Thus Jung came to understand that the central concept of his work was the process of individuation.

As mentioned earlier, the impulse for individuation comes from the archetype of the Self, which tries to guide a person toward wholeness in order to live his or her unique destiny. Barbara Hannah believes that "in every living creature the urge for its own totality is perhaps the strongest and most fundamental of all urges," and when this urge has been violated for too long, there is "suffering from homesickness for a more balanced natural condition."[153] For some, this leads to the secret garden of analysis. This is not an idyllic situation with a certain outcome. Hannah speaks about the difficulties of reclaiming fragments and discarded elements of the psyche as well as the responsibility involved:

> To regain the personal elements that have been discarded all our lives is usually very discouraging and painful work. We would not have thrown them away (and subsequently forgotten about them) had we recognized

---

150 *We: Understanding the Psychology of Romantic Love*, p. 171.

151 *Psychology and Alchemy*, CW 12, par. 63.

152 *Memories, Dreams, Reflections*, p. 196.

153 *Striving Towards Wholeness*, pp. 4f.

Figure 8. Mandala by C.G. Jung.

their value; even if they are positive in themselves, we had our reasons for discarding them. Good qualities and talents spell responsibility and hard work and, if we regain them, we shall have to overcome a great deal of laziness and fear.[154]

The individuation process fosters a relationship between the ego and unconscious material generated by the Self in the form of dreams, art, fantasy and active imagination, so it can be contemplated and possibly integrated into the personality. This constitutes the psychological work of finding the pearl of great price.[155] It can be fostered in the temenos, the secret garden, of analysis.

Analysis as Temenos for Individuation

One of the difficulties in speaking about analysis in a world dominated by collective concepts is its uniqueness for each individual. Jung says he was often asked about his analytic method but found it difficult to reply because it was different for everyone:

> Psychotherapy and analysis are as varied as are human individuals. I treat every patient as individually as possible, because the solution of the problem is always an individual one. . . .
>   . . . In my analyses . . . I am unsystematic very much by intention. To my mind, in dealing with individuals, only individual understanding will do. We need a different language for every patient.[156]

Self-knowledge comes from one's own unconscious as it reveals itself. Analysis is a gradual process of revelation, assimilation and transformation, undertaken with another person, such as a trained analyst, who has been on the journey. Gradually, one connects with previously unknown facets of the personality that enrich or restart the flow of life.

Jung considers the outcome of analysis as a state of being in balance

---

[154] Ibid., p. 19.

[155] "The kingdom of heaven is like unto a merchant man, seeking goodly pearls: who, when he had found one pearl of great price, went and sold all that he had, and bought it." (Matt. 13:45-46; Authorized King James Version)

[156] *Memories, Dreams, Reflections*, p. 131.

with one's own nature. This is never a fixed state, but requires sensitivity to the ebb and flow of life.

> Through the assimilation of unconscious contents, the momentary life of consciousness can once more be brought into harmony with the law of nature from which it all too easily departs, and the [person] can be led back to the natural law of his own being.[157]

This process goes beyond the notion of cure. Jung's remark, quoted earlier, is worth repeating:

> It leads in the end to that distant goal which may perhaps have been the first urge to life: the complete actualization of the whole human being, that is, individuation.[158]

There are no universally established criteria for suitable outcomes. The point, writes von Franz, is "to help the patient hear better what the patient's own psyche is whispering to him."[159] Needless to say, at times this is at odds with the current emphasis on objectively observable data as an indication of the efficacy of therapy.

Analysis is indeed a deeply private affair. As Jung says:

> What happens within oneself when one integrates previously unconscious contents with the consciousness is something which can scarcely be described in words. It can only be experienced. It is a subjective affair quite beyond discussion; we have a particular feeling about ourselves, about the way we are, and that is a fact which it is neither possible nor meaningful to doubt. . . . Whether a change has taken place as the result of integration, and what the nature of that change is, remains a matter of subjective conviction. To be sure, it is not a fact which can be scientifically verified and therefore finds no place in an official view of the world.[160]

Indeed, changes may be very subtle, discernible only by taking the long, retrospective view.

---

157 "The Practical Use of Dream-Analysis," *The Practice of Psychotherapy*, CW 16, par. 351.

158 Ibid., par. 352.

159 "The Religious Dimension of Analysis," in *Psychotherapy*, p. 179.

160 *Memories, Dreams, Reflections*, p. 287.

In the temenos of the secret garden of analysis, there is an attitude of care and attentiveness to that which is emerging and particularly to discovering the essence of the dreams. This requires separation from the habitual routine of life, usually for a period of one or two hours a week. Such separation, notes Françoise O'Kane, is the first stage in a ritual "whose function it is to structure time and create life."[161] It is a necessary precursor to a period of marginality or the liminal phase to follow. This is where the secret garden is located.

After the requisite initial stage of separation, the ritual of analysis occurs in the liminal phase and space. Here, in this second stage, "a reality that is outside society and culture—and outside ego life—is experienced. Deep values and emotions are brought into the open."[162] The transformative energy of Eros and the transcendent function within the psyche can emerge into the field of conscious experience.

There is an atmosphere of deep concentration in the liminal phase. One can dwell in the presence of the numinous symbols of dreams. This can be strengthening to a person, enabling a passage from one state to another through the contemplation of the symbols and the integration of their meaning into consciousness.

The foundation of ritual is an acknowledgment of the relationship between destruction and creation, loss and gain, death and rebirth. Thus, ritual can function as a supportive bridge between one level of consciousness and another. It is also a vehicle that helps to strengthen the ego sufficiently to hold the tension of the opposites, to tolerate the accompanying uncertainty, even disorientation. The children working in the secret garden were in a liminal space. As it was for them, in the temenos of analysis there is space and time to discover the rhythms of one's own nature and to establish a connection with remote aspects of the psyche. For some people it also facilitates a reconnection with their historical, cultural and ancestral roots.

This liminal space is between, yet joins, the material with the spiritual life, the sacred with the profane, the immanent with the transcendent. All

---

[161] *Sacred Chaos,* p. 44.

[162] Ibid., p. 45.

the functions of consciousness (thinking, feeling, sensation and intuition) are engaged in receiving expressions of the unconscious. Separation from daily life and the desire for change make this possible. The analytic hour is protected from the influences of the outer world and also values intimate material from the depths of the unconscious.

Analysis can be a safe place for a descent. In the ancient world, when a difficult situation arose which could not be solved by ordinary means, an individual would go to an oracle, such as at Delphi, a place of secret revelation. The information and experience which came from the unknown depths constituted an initiation into a deeper realm. Therefore it occurred in a separate place, a temenos, often below the surface of the earth. Similarly, in analysis there is a descent below the surface of ego consciousness not only to find answers but, more than that, for an experience of the truth about oneself.

"To let the unconscious go its own way and to experience it as a reality," notes Jung, "is something that exceeds the courage and capacity" of many people.[163] But the protecting temenos of the analytic relationship makes it possible if one is truly called to do this work.

Recall Jung's remark that the knowledge gained by one's experience of the unconscious "is a personal secret communicable only to very few, and that with difficulty; hence the isolating effect."[164] He also said that the unconscious "should not be subordinated to the rationalistic judgments of consciousness."[165] This is difficult for the intellect to accept, so it may protest. The conflict cannot be resolved by understanding, only by experience:

> Every stage of the experience must be lived through. There is no feat of interpretation or any other trick by which to circumvent this difficulty, for the union of conscious and unconscious can only be achieved step by step.[166]

---

[163] *Psychology and Alchemy,* CW 12, par. 60.

[164] Ibid., par. 61.

[165] Ibid., par. 59.

[166] Ibid.

What does one do with this life-changing inner experience, this pearl of great price? It is most important to hold it close, nor should one speak of it to those who would scoff. Inner experience needs to be preserved within a container, otherwise its essence can be dissipated or exploited, or both.

What is a suitable container? Von Franz writes:

> The inner experience has to be preserved and to have a frame. What would be the best frame? Instinct advises the simplest thing, namely to keep it secret and inconspicuous and invisible to the outside. . . . Ambition, or ego restlessness which has not been integrated, will never accept that, but, through such mistakes, will destroy the inner experience.[167]

The secret of inner experience has a vitality which can be transformative if it is lived, rather than divulged far and wide, which robs it of its numinosity.[168]

> The quality of sacredness consists not only in what is there in the inner world, but also in the attitude we take toward it. . . . It is up to us to recognize it, treat it as the sacred, in order to experience its power.[169]

Kairos, Sacred Time

The atmosphere of openness that can develop in the temenos of analysis often engenders a unique experience of time. There is fluidity between past, present and future, along with a heightened aliveness in the moment. One of my dreams spoke to me of this special quality of time:

> I met some people at a gathering. We decided to attend a Christmas Eve service which was to begin shortly at a nearby church. It would take a few minutes to get there so we did not have much time. Nevertheless, before we left there were several things I had to do.
>
> I had to go down into the basement of the building to find something. I

---

[167] *Individuation in Fairy Tales,* p. 149.

[168] One of the teachings of Jesus is the value of secrets. He counsels that when you pray, "go into a room by yourself, shut the door, and pray to your Father who is there in the secret place; and your Father who sees what is secret will reward you" (Matt. 6:6; New English Bible)

[169] Johnson, *We,* p. 175.

found several objects quite quickly, but these were not what I was really looking for. There was something else, but I was not sure what it was. Eventually I found it. I knew as soon as I saw it: this was *it!*

It was an exquisite little clock which was also a piece of jewelry—a brooch. The face of the clock was a delicate peach cameo. The head, in profile, was of a lovely, young woman, very gracefully and precisely rendered. There were diamonds and pearls surrounding the clock. The hours and minutes were all designated by tiny bars of gold. It was very old. The cameo was so finely carved it almost seemed alive. There was an arresting quality to the piece. It was really breathtaking.

I took it upstairs to show the people I was with. Mrs. W. was there. She said it did not belong to her and besides, she would never buy such an object because it was not her taste. I was totally surprised by this response because, to me, the clock was so stunningly lovely that it was beyond personal taste. It seemed to express something very deep which it did perfectly. It produced a sense of wonder in me, not judgment.

I thought someone must have lost it. I searched but there was no owner. Then it appeared that it was meant for me. I was to keep this treasure safely myself.

This dream came to me almost on my birthday, a day when I am particularly sensitive to the passage of time, as well as appreciative of the gift of life. Christmas is the point in the Christian liturgical year when the birth of the holy child is celebrated. In psychological terms this could be considered the birth of new consciousness.

Evidently I could not go immediately to this celebration with the group, even though it meant that I would almost certainly be late. In order for the experience to be meaningful, I had to find something else, but I did not know what that was. I had to search, to make a descent, to get away from the collective group, and to be alone in order to find what was essential for my progress. Fortunately, I recognized it when I found it.

A clock is a symbol of wholeness, a mandala. This particular clock had a woman's face on it, indicating a feminine quality of time flowing in a connected way, rather than a time-management tool. In the dream I value it when I find it, whereas Mrs. W. does not. The dream caused me to wonder if this is the quality of time I bring to the analytic work, as well as to my own life as I grow older. The dream seemed to open up an appreciation of the quality of time present.

This may have been an effort by the unconscious to compensate my conscious worries about how quickly the years seem to fly away. But not necessarily the minutes. There are boundary markings on the clock but each is marked in gold, the eternal, incorruptible substance. The whole is surrounded by precious and semiprecious stones. Within this mandala and temenos there is a unique, graceful, soul quality to time which cannot be appreciated by everyone; rather it is a special gift meant for a specific person.

I find that often the present moment within each analytic hour has a heightened clarity that ordinary time does not. There are many sessions when all dimensions seem to be constellated: the past suddenly becomes alive because of a painful recollection or a healing memory; the future is also present as the symbolic material of the dream is pondered and reveals the gradient in which the psychic energy needs to flow. The analytic hour can seem much longer or shorter than actual clock time.

This special quality of time in the temenos of analysis is suggested to me in the poem "Fern Hill" by Dylan Thomas:

> And the sabbath rang slowly
> In the pebbles of the holy streams.[170]

It is not only the past, present and future aspects of time that can be constellated, but also the fourth dimension, the eternal.

According to the philosopher Jean Gebser, this perception of all dimensions of time simultaneously is an arational-integral consciousness of the "ever-present origin" as a reality from which every moment of our lives draws its sustenance, and it is "by nature divine and spiritual."[171] This integral consciousness embraces all time as a living present. Gebser considers it to be a new, emerging form of consciousness, possible only "through an insightful process of intensive awareness."[172] But like the

---

[170] *Norton Anthology of English Literature,* vol. 2, p. 2285.

[171] *The Ever-Present Origin,* p. 530.

[172] Ibid., p. 6.

experiential knowledge gained in analysis, "it cannot be striven for, only elicited or awakened."[173]

Sometimes the redeeming quality of time will be constellated in a dream. An aspect of the past seems so alive in a new form that all coalesces in the "Now-moment," which according to Meister Eckhart contains all time.[174] It is redeeming because it brings a new perception. A dream I had years ago on Easter Sunday illustrates this phenomenon:

> I was in a large old house which was being renovated. Everything was a mess and I was too exhausted to care. I had never known myself to be so exhausted. I had more or less lost track of time. But on the way to my bedroom I noticed something wonderful happening in the garden.
>
> There was a banquet being prepared. The garden was festooned with colored lanterns and a large table was set, laden with food. It was off in a special part of the garden, enclosed by trees and flowers, so it was very secluded. Everything was so beautiful over there—quite different from the general situation in which I was living.
>
> Then it dawned on me that this was my birthday. This realization came to me as if it were penetrating from a great distance. I had sunk a long way from caring about such things because I had become so engulfed in trying to cope with the practicalities of my life.
>
> Further, I realized that my parents were in the garden preparing this wonderful surprise birthday for me. I was deeply moved by this. I wept with gratitude that they would celebrate me like this, even from the other side. I knew they wanted this celebration to be a surprise. I resolved to not let on that I knew about it.

The discovery of this surprise birthday party in the garden touched me in a manner I had not felt for a long time. The dream reached into my heaviness and despondency with sparks of hope and joy. It was truly a resurrection dream wherein time past redeemed time present to bring new life. It gave me a vision of being cherished now from the depths, reminding me of my parents' abiding love. This reality seemed to have been eclipsed by my struggles since their deaths years before.

---

[173] Ibid., p. 300.

[174] See Robert B. Blakney, trans., *Meister Eckhart*, p. 212.

To pursue individuation one must ask, "What is it, at this moment and in this individual, that represents the natural urge of life? That is the question."[175] When people asked Jung, "What can I do?" he would reply,

> "Become what you have always been," namely, the wholeness which we have lost in the midst of our civilized, conscious existence, a wholeness which we always were without knowing it.[176]

One is led in this discovery by receiving and valuing the symbols created by the psyche itself. It means paying attention to these creations now, not at some future point that might be more convenient. They often slip away, forgotten, by then. Since the garden is a part of earth with its seasons, it has a cyclical progression. Each stage is a valuable phase in the whole pattern. Fulfillment is not only in the harvest but in all its stages. As St. Paul says, "Behold, now *is* the accepted time; behold, now *is* the day of salvation." (2 Cor. 6:2; Authorized King James Version).

According to Northrop Frye, *kairos* is "the sudden critical widening of the present moment."[177] It is as if the divine has radically intercepted human time so that some crucial awareness may enter life. For Meister Eckhart the "eternal now-moment" comes from God within the soul.[178] It seems to originate in a realm experienced as sacred and profoundly significant, possibly even a turning point in life. This does not occur through personal will. Rather, it is as if a divine decision makes a special time and place crucial for the transformation of an individual.

Oscar Cullman, a New Testament scholar, speaks of it as integral to "God's plan of salvation."[179] He considers *kairos* to be an experience of time that is redeeming, consisting of unique moments of ultimate significance. "Not all fragments of ongoing time constitute redemptive history . . . but rather these specific points, these *kairoi*, singled out from time as a whole."[180]

---

[175] *Two Essays,* CW 7, par. 488.

[176] "Flying Saucers: A Modern Myth," *Civilization in Transition,* CW 10, par. 722.

[177] *The Double Vision,* p. 55.

[178] Blakney, trans., *Meister Eckhart,* p. 209.

[179] *Christ and Time,* p. 39.

[180] Ibid., p. 40.

The experience of a sacred moment, *kairos*, often presents a special psychological opportunity for the next step in one's development. If this chance is missed, a depression may follow, because the urge moving one toward wholeness has been denied. Von Franz writes:

[There is] a fairytale motif in which a valuable flower blossoms every nine years out of a pond, or the earth, and if one misses this moment, then one must wait another nine years for the next chance. There are those numinous moments of possible realization, and if one misses them it is over.[181]

As an example of this, von Franz tells of a man who fell in love with a woman but for ethical reasons did not pursue the relationship. During this period of reserve, his dreams were very disturbing. Eventually a voice told him in a dream, "If one misses certain things at a certain moment, one has missed one's whole life." He was so shaken that he was spurred to action. Von Franz comments that there are these moments— one could say sacred moments—

where one knows that if one is now a coward . . . one will not get the chance again for a very long time. The unconscious generally makes that quite clear and because things have not reached consciousness we have this terrible comedown after.[182]

Pip, the narrator in Dickens' novel *Great Expectations*, reflects on one special time which was the turning point of his life. He then leaps out of the narrative, urging the reader to similarly reflect:

That was a memorable day to me, for it made great changes in me. But it is the same with any life. Imagine one selected day struck out of it, and think how different its course would have been. Pause you who read this, and think for a moment of the long chain of iron or gold, of thorns or of flowers, that would never have bound you, but for the formation of the first link on one memorable day.[183]

When one grasps that there is a unique process occurring within, a

---

[181] *Golden Ass,* p. 145.

[182] Ibid., pp. 145f.

[183] *Great Expectations,* p. 70.

process meant specifically for one's personal fulfillment, it is a profound moment. It becomes apparent that each life is embedded somewhere, in realms that cannot be understood. The realization of this otherness inside can be a welcome light for the long journey. Knowing that one is not alone inside one's own skin, that life is grounded in unknown soil, and that one is participating in a great mystery, can be a deeply moving, even healing experience. The soul can thrive in that knowledge and the spirit can be received again. Thereby one may glimpse some dimension of truth in the statement from Revelation: "To everyone who conquers, I will give permission to eat from the tree of life that is in the paradise of God." (Rev. 2:7)

Gardening in Analysis

The work carried out in *The Secret Garden* parallels the work of analysis. It is not ruthless pursuit of a specific goal. Rather, it is a process of exploration often initiated by deep distress. The first task is to find the buried key to the locked door. The Self may have been knocking at the door long before the ego could respond. An image of this can be seen in the Book of Revelation:

> Behold, I stand at the door and knock: if any man hear my voice, and open the door, I will come in to him, and will sup with him, and he with me. (Rev. 3:20; Authorized King James Version)

After one gains entry to the secret garden, the work is guided by developing a relationship with what is found there, as in the story:

> Mary was very much absorbed, indeed. . . . She found many more of the sprouting pale green points than she had ever hoped to find. They seemed to be starting up everywhere and each day she was sure she found tiny new ones, some so tiny that they barely peeped through the earth.

In the quietude of analysis, the "green points" from the symbolic world of the psyche gradually gain strength. New growth comes, or not, according to its own timing. Even before my adult interest in *The Secret Garden* became clear to me, an image of green points, or shoots as I called them, appeared in one of my dreams. Here it is, along with my subsequent reflections:

> My parents had a second house. When we went to check that everything
> was all right with it, we found a lot of things in the basement that still
> needed to be sorted and moved. I was quite depressed about it. This was
> another huge task and there was no place in my present home for any
> more. To my surprise there were many large pots of plants—geraniums I
> think—that had been stored in the cellar for years. Despite being totally
> neglected there were lots of green shoots sprouting up. I was moved by
> their determination to live. I wondered where I could put them so that they
> would thrive. I wanted them not only to live but to thrive.

It seemed to me that a part of my life which had been neglected
wanted to live. The green shoots still had the urge for life. In the dream I
am going to take care of them to the best of my ability, but likely dispose
of everything else. This dream image reminded me of the phenomenon of
"greening power," or *viriditas,* the term used by Hildegard of Bingen, a
twelfth-century Christian mystic. One commentator writes that for her,

> the Holy Spirit is greening power in motion, making all things grow, ex-
> pand, celebrate. Indeed for Hildegard salvation or healing is the return of
> greening power and moistness. . . . What else is *viriditas?* It is God's
> freshness that humans receive in their spiritual and physical life-forces. It
> is the power of springtime, a germinating force, a fruitfulness that comes
> from God and permeates all creation. . . . The tragedy of drying up and ig-
> noring the greening power is that nothing is created.[184]

Early in my analytic journey, before I knew its riches, I still searched
in books for knowledge concerning matters of the soul. This did not yield
anything that corresponded to my heart's desire. Then I had this dream:

> I was in a bookstore. All the plants were drying up and dying. I went to get
> some water. The pump was in the trunk of a tree. So I started to pump
> water from the tree. I had to bring the water up from very deep in the
> earth—it was *very* far away. I wondered if it might even be salty because
> it might be from the ocean. When the water started to flow out of the tree,
> I realized it was coming from a place even further than the ocean because

---

[184] Matthew Fox, ed., *Illuminations of Hildegard of Bingen,* pp. 30ff.

it was incredibly pure. It was important to keep the pump primed now that this pure water was flowing from it. The plants were starting to turn green.

The water in the dream reminded me of the well of living water mentioned in the Gospel of John:

> Whosoever drinketh of the water that I shall give him shall never thirst; but the water that I shall give him shall be in him a well of water springing up into everlasting life. (John 4:14; Authorized King James Version)

The most important task is to keep this pump primed because it has a connection to the Self. In my dream it was akin to "a pure river of water of life, clear as crystal, proceeding out of the throne of God and of the Lamb." (Rev. 22:1; Authorized King James Version) This, to my mind, is the source of *viriditas* and transformative knowledge.

In *Mysterium Coniunctionis,* Jung quotes alchemical writers on the *benedicta viriditas,* "the blessed greenness which generates all things":

> God breathed into created things . . . a certain germination or greenness, by which all things should multiply . . . They called all things green, for to be green means to grow . . . Therefore this virtue of generation and the preservation of things might be called the Soul of the World.[185]

Another example of *viriditas* in the psyche is Jung's dream of the green Christ:

> One night I awoke and saw, bathed in bright light at the foot of my bed, the figure of Christ on the cross. It was not quite life-size, but extremely distinct; and I saw that his body was made of greenish gold. The vision was marvellously beautiful, and yet I was profoundly shaken by it.[186]

Reflecting upon this dream, he recognized the green gold, understood alchemically, as the living quality in both man and inorganic nature. This vision depicted a union of the Christ-image with matter, "a union of

---

[185] CW 14, par. 623. (Edward F. Edinger: "I keep a permanent marker here in *Mysterium.* I call it the 'blessed greenness' page, and whenever a dream comes up involving the color green I take that page out and read it."—*The Mysterium Lectures: A Journey through C.G. Jung's* Mysterium Coniunctionis, p. 269.)

[186] *Memories, Dreams, Reflections,* p. 210.

spiritually alive and physically dead matter."[187]

In *The Secret Garden,* one of the first lessons Mary wanted to learn from Dickon was how to distinguish between the living and the dead plants. He explained that if there is green in the wood it is alive.

> They went from bush to bush and from tree to tree. He was very strong and clever with his knife and knew how to cut the dry and dead wood away, and could tell when an unpromising bough or twig had still green life in it.

The living wood can be choked if the dead is not cleared away. Pruning also helps to strengthen the roots. Mary had intuitively made "little clearings round the pale green points," in order to make space for them.

Discriminating between the living and the dead wood in one's life can be very difficult. Often a person is very attached to the dead wood, whatever that may be. Sometimes there is the desire to keep everything rather than experience the pain of clearing out whatever is choking new potential. There may be so much happening in a person's life, so many new green shoots coming through that none really has a chance to become strong. Again, Mary's intuitive impulse to clear the ground to make room for new growth is instructive. In analysis also there may be many new developments. Discernment is required in order to know what is calling for attention, needing space to be cleared for it to develop.

This may be experienced as loss. But death was the precipitating factor instigating the circumstances which led to renewal in *The Secret Garden*. Psychologically this can be understood as the difficult process of giving up ego attitudes to which one is attached, in order to have a deeper connection to the new life that is trying to break through.

Jung makes a very significant statement:

> It is . . . impossible to achieve individuation by conscious intention, because conscious intention invariably leads to a typical attitude that excludes whatever does not fit in with it.[188]

---

[187] Ibid., p. 211.

[188] *Two Essays,* CW 7, par. 505.

A Propitious Attitude

Many of the qualities the children had in relation to the secret garden are similar to those required in analysis. They were devoted to their project, not from a slavish sense of duty or rigid expectations about the outcome, but with interest and excitement about how the garden would develop. Their attitude was "propitious": it fostered the process. There was no attempt to dominate it. They watched the garden to see what was needed as they participated in its mystery.

This experience was the inspiration, the inner fire, for their work. They prepared the soil, planted seeds, pruned the old growth to create space for the new. They were favorably disposed to their project. Similarly, in the rhythm of the analytic process there is a special time for the planting of the seeds, for the harvest, and for incorporating into life what one has learned. The garden of analysis, a unique aspect of a natural process, is a container open to the transcendent, bringing with it an experience of the depth of one's life. For this to happen, a supportive, propitious attitude is required.

A propitious attitude is also a pragmatic one, so that the unconscious can cooperate with consciousness rather than being driven into opposition.[189] Underlying this attitude is respect for the creative capacity of the psyche. Genuine healing comes when the ego, with the right attitude, finds a relationship with those aspects of the Self which complete it.

> It is important to understand that should "healing" take place, it will depend more on an attitude than on an answer. It will rest on experience, including mistakes and detours, rather than on a definition of a clear-cut path.[190]

In our story, the children worked diligently, but it was a time of such creativity that it seemed more like play. When Mary first thought of her project she shyly said, "I—I want to play that—that I have a garden of my own. . . . I—there is nothing for me to do. I have nothing—and no one." When she first meets her guardian, Archie Craven, he asks what

---

[189] O'Kane, *Sacred Chaos,* p. 17.
[190] Ibid., p. 31.

she wants to do. She answers, "I want to play out of doors." She explains, "It makes me feel strong when I play and the wind comes over the moor." He inquires, "Where do you play?" She responds, "Everywhere. . . . I skip and run and I look about to see if things are beginning to stick out of the earth."

Then she bravely asks, "Might I have a bit of earth? . . . To plant seeds in—to make things grow—to see them come alive." When Dickon first sees the garden with Mary, he observes, "There's a lot of work to do here!" But he is also so excited by the project ahead that he declares, "It's the best fun I ever had in my life—shut in here an' wakenin' up a garden. . . . We'll have a lot o' fun."

Mary's awakening to her desire to play is one of the endearing developments in the story. A childhood devoid of play seems unbearably bleak. Play engenders enthusiasm, energy, fellowship, even creativity. All of this becomes accessible for life. Then sometimes the difference between play and work becomes blurred. The project at hand is so radiant with the Eros of exploration, discovery and connectedness that it is in itself the fullness of life. Such a process has its own momentum and vitality, bringing with it a sense of purpose and belonging. This was a huge gift for Mary and Colin who had both been lost and did not seem to belong anywhere. All the children were passionately engaged in their secret gardening.

Similarly, analytic work can be enlivened by the creative Eros of play bestowing its gift of surprising growth in unexpected places. The spontaneity and astonishing diversity of the unconscious often invite a certain playfulness. Thus the absorbing, serious nature of the work can be tempered with a spirit of play which is also creative. This is one of the beauties of the secret garden of analysis. There is a place to notice the nuances of life. Everything may seem, like the garden in the story, "strange and silent and . . . hundreds of miles away from anyone." But there is a deep satisfaction in realizing that one can go there to cultivate, witness and integrate the images coming into consciousness.

Indeed, an important catalyst for the developments in the story is the experience of being seen, mirrored by another, which in turn fosters the ability to see others and become aware of oneself in relation to the world. Martha's frank observations of Mary stimulated her development. Later the robin and the old gardener, Ben Weatherstaff, did the same. He talked to her in such an odd way that Mary wondered if he was actually a little sorry for her.

> She had never felt sorry for herself; she had only felt tired and cross, because she disliked people and things so much. But now the world seemed to be changing and getting nicer.

Similarly, learning to mirror the unconscious in consciousness is one of the tasks in analysis. It is important to learn the art of seeing so that what has been lying beneath the surface, affecting one's life in various untoward ways, can be witnessed. Then connections can be made. Jung wrote eloquently about this:

> It is high time we realized that it is pointless to praise the light and preach it if nobody can see it. It is much more needful to teach people the art of seeing. For it is obvious that far too many people are incapable of establishing a connection between the sacred figures and their own psyche: they cannot see to what extent the equivalent images are lying dormant in their own unconscious. In order to facilitate this inner vision we must first clear the way for the faculty of seeing. How this is to be done without psychology, that is, without making contact with the psyche, is frankly beyond my comprehension.[191]

Dickon had a useful criterion for the children's gardening:

> "I wouldn't want to make it look like a gardener's garden, all clipped an' spick an' span, would you?" he said. "It's nicer like this with things runnin' wild, an' swingin' an' catching' hold of each other." "Don't let us make it tidy," said Mary anxiously. "It wouldn't seem like a secret garden if it was tidy."

Working with unconscious material is similar. It cannot be all clipped and tidy. There is no routine procedure ensuring a neat outcome. Instead, it has to be left a bit wild, with things swinging and catching hold of each other, because that is the nature of the archetypal world of the psyche.

---

[191] *Psychology and Alchemy,* CW 12, par. 14.

Plant Symbolism and Psychological Growth

Often the unconscious uses plant symbolism to convey its revelations. It is important to give a symbol space through thoughtful contemplation of its possible meanings. Jung tried to understand each image that arose in him, and to realize its implications for his life, an often neglected step:

> We allow the images to rise up, and maybe we wonder about them, but that is all. We do not take the trouble to understand them, let alone draw ethical conclusions from them. This stopping-short conjures up the negative effects of the unconscious.[192]

Failure to understand the images from one's unconscious, or ignoring the ethical implications, deprives a person of wholeness, imposing a "painful fragmentariness on . . . life."[193]

A plant can be seen as a symbol for psychological as well as spiritual growth. The union of spirit and matter can be appreciated in the partnership between plants and animals. Since animals feed on plants, their life force is also within us. The plant can be considered like a spiritual dimension supporting life from within.

Plants feed on the four elements—earth, air, water and the fire of the sun. They are independent of animals. Their growth is a seasonal, cyclical oscillation. A tree continues to blossom and bear fruit until it dies. Thus the life of a plant could be considered less chaotic, less violent than human or animal life. Human life would be less violent if it were firmly rooted in the earth.

In *The Perfection of the Morning,* Sharon Butala recounts a healing dream which for her had spiritual as well as psychological significance:

> In mid-July 1986 I dreamt I opened a book a friend had given me and inside it I found an old, pressed twig. As I watched, the twig grew full and round, its leaves unfolded and swelled and turned green and it became a branch. Then one by one, three trumpet-shaped, blue flowers sprang out on it and blossomed to fullness.[194]

---

[192] *Memories, Dreams, Reflections*, p. 192.

[193] Ibid., p. 193.

[194] *The Perfection of the Morning*, p. 155.

Upon waking, she spent time thinking of mythical associations to the symbol of the twig. She says,

> I awoke and thought of Aaron's magical rod that brought plagues to the Egyptians, of the golden branch hung with bells the Irish poets—ollaves— carried with them in honour of Brigit, Goddess of Poets, of the Golden Bough Aeneas plucked from a tree and carried into the underworld, which made it possible for him to return to the upper world . . . , of Gilgamesh who, with great hardship, went down to the bottom of the cosmic sea to collect the branch of Immortal Life. I thought of the ancient and recurring symbol of the Tree of Life.[195]

Then she began to ponder what this image might mean for her personally. She turned to Jung for this. She tells us,

> I searched through my books for an interpretation on a level more clearly a part of my daily life and found this in Jung's *Man and His Symbols*: "An ancient tree or plant represents symbolically the growth and development of psychic life [as distinct from instinctual life commonly symbolized by animals]."[196]

Reflecting upon all this, she found the meaning for her:

> I took this as a sign that I was nearing the edge of the forest, that whatever I had been through in my crisis was resolving itself, that I had survived these trials and that things would begin to be easier, clearer, simpler, although I could not see how, nor any reason why they should.[197]

Jung explains further that a plant symbolizes new developments because it grows in a manner that parallels the growth of the psyche:

> In plants the buds or the beginnings of leaves are arranged in a spiral, a plant grows in a spiral. . . . it is the functioning of opposites, the reconciliation of opposites. The man who discovered the mathematical law of the spiral is buried in my native town, in Basel; on his tombstone is a spiral with this device, EADEM MUTATA RESURGO, literally translated,

---

[195] Ibid.
[196] Ibid.
[197] Ibid.

"in an identical way, changed, I lift myself up" That is the law of the spiral, a very beautiful thing. . . . Sameness, non-sameness. . . . So the spiral is really a very apt symbol to express development.[198]

Figure 9. Spiral structure of a rose blossom.

---

[198] Jung, *Visions Seminars,* vol. 1, pp. 95f.

The psyche as a whole has the same spiral, rhythmic, cyclical growth as a garden, as does the development of consciousness. The ego will often make value judgments about these slow developments, but if the unconscious is permitted to reveal itself gradually to a caring ego, then one may be able to win through to a loving awareness of one's personal grounding in the archetypal world.

From his study of alchemy, Jung realized that

the unconscious is a *process*, and that the psyche is transformed or developed by the relationship of the ego to the contents of the unconscious. In individual cases that transformation can be read from dreams and fantasies. In collective life it has left its deposit principally in the various religious systems and their changing symbols.[199]

Dreams are invariably an important part of the experience of the unconscious in analysis. Their interpretation touches the imagination and the realm of story. Jung's view of dreams is clear:

The dream is a little hidden door in the innermost and most secret recesses of the soul, opening into that cosmic night which was psyche long before there was any ego-consciousness, and which will remain psyche no matter how far our ego-consciousness extends. . . . All consciousness separates; but in dreams we put on the likeness of that more universal, truer, more eternal man dwelling in the darkness of primordial night. There he is still the whole, and the whole is in him, indistinguishable from nature and bare of all egohood.

It is from these all-uniting depths that the dream arises, be it ever so childish, grotesque, and immoral. So flowerlike is it in its candour and veracity that it makes us blush for the deceitfulness of our lives. No wonder that in all the ancient civilizations an impressive dream was accounted a message from the gods![200]

What is the key to this dream-door which is also the hidden door to the unconscious? Each of us has our own key to the inner personality

---

[199] *Memories, Dreams, Reflections*, p. 209.

[200] "The Meaning of Psychology for Modern Man," *Civilization in Transition,* CW 10, pars. 304f.

which is as if locked in a chest, or buried in the ground as it was in *The Secret Garden*. This inner personality cannot be reached without the key.

When the interpretation of a dream resonates for the dreamer, the key has been found; there is a sense of opening to what has been locked away. It is an "Aha!" feeling. Von Franz writes:

> Every understood dream is like a slight electric shock into higher consciousness; normally one has the feeling, "Oh, now I understand," and that has a vivifying effect.[201]

The interpretation of a dream is not a mechanical formula, though this notion is fostered by the plethora of books offering simple, systematic, do-it-yourself outlines for dream interpretation. Rather, it reflects the uniqueness of the dreamer. When the life experiences, memories, feelings and, where appropriate, the relevant archetypal amplification profoundly touches the dreamer, then the key has been found This is deeply satisfying; it is a drop of psychological gold which nourishes the soul. As St. Ignatius of Loyola says, "It is not an abundance of knowledge that fills and satisfies the soul but rather an interior understanding and savouring of things."[202]

Jung considers dreams, like plants, as a natural aspect of God's world:

> To me dreams are a part of nature, which harbors no intention to deceive, but expresses something as best it can, just as a plant grows or an animal seeks its food as best it can. These forms of life, too, have no wish to deceive our eyes, but we may deceive ourselves because our eyes are shortsighted. Or we may hear amiss because our ears are rather deaf.[203]

Part of the gardening work in analysis is understanding the hidden meaning of these living beings, the dreams, as they flower. They are the light in the darkness of the unconscious. This is the *lumen naturae,* the "light in nature," of the alchemists. Jung describes it:

> The *lumen naturae* is the light of the darkness itself, which illuminates its own darkness, and this light the darkness comprehends. Therefore it turns

---

[201] *Alchemical Active Imagination*, p. 72.

[202] *The Spiritual Exercises of St. Ignatius*, p. 37.

[203] *Memories, Dreams, Reflections*, pp. 161f.

blackness into brightness, burns away "all superfluities."[204]

The psyche is lit by its own light. As the Gospel of John says, "The light shines in the darkness, and the darkness did not overcome it." (John 1:5) Circumambulation of this light with respect, humility and an open mind is an important dimension of the individuation process in the secret garden of analysis. If the dreams can be understood in a meaningful way, there is a satisfaction and an opening to possibilities. Consciousness is lit by the light of the unconscious. This is how self-knowledge develops.

This *lumen naturae*, the light of nature, or in psychological terms, the light in the darkness of the unconscious, can sometimes be seen symbolically in dreams. One example is my dream of the Dark Woman recounted in chapter two. Years later I had the following dream, which I titled "Light in Nature":

> I met some people at the hairdresser's. I invited them to my place for a visit. We walked to my apartment. When I opened the door I was struck by how totally fascinating it was to me. It seemed that I was discovering the place for myself in a new way. It was quite amazing to me.
>
> First of all I could see that there was a *very* long hallway leading to a conservatory in the distance. There were masses of lush green plants and trees at the end of the hall and in the conservatory. Even in the main room close to the front door there were lots of green plants along with various interesting artifacts.
>
> But the main feature which became apparent to me and riveted my attention was a wonderful candelabra made from the roots of a tree. There were tiny receptacles all over the roots for holding candles. There was a lot of wax from the burning candles. I mean, this was not just a candelabra to be looked at. It had been used a lot and was meant to be used. I put fresh candles in the receptacles and lit them. The whole place became breathtakingly lovely in the candlelight. It gave a special radiance. As I gazed at the sight I knew that this was an important symbol for my soul and my life.

For me, the central symbol of the roots of the tree also being a candelabra is a union of earth and heaven. Evidently this mystical tree had al-

---

204 "Paracelsus as a Spiritual Phenomenon," *Alchemical Studies,* CW 13, par. 197.

ways been there, but I had not really seen it before. It seemed that now my life was to be in the service of this light in nature, the light in the darkness of the unconscious, which is also a part of my everyday world.

Joseph Campbell notes that dreams come from the same depths as myth, but access to their reality has largely been lost:

> In myth, as in dream, it is the secret of the inner world that comes to us, but the deepest secret, and from the profundities too dreadful to be lightly known. Out of our own depths arise the forms; but out of regions where man is still terrible in wisdom, beauty, and bliss. This Atlantis of the interior realities is as strange to us as a foreign continent. Its secret must be learned. And the way of learning is not that of laboratory and lecture hall, but of controlled introspection.[205]

Figure 10. Garden of daisies.

---

[205] "The Art of Reading Myths," quoted in Stephen Larsen and Robin Larsen, *A Fire in the Mind: The Life of Joseph Campbell,* p. 338.

6
Cultural and Psychological Implications

As discussed earlier, archetypes are living ideas or energy systems within the matrix of the collective unconscious; they continually express themselves by various means, both in an individual psyche, through complexes, and collectively, as characteristics of whole cultures.

Thus archetypes have a universal quality, capable of infinite variety in their manifestations. But there is a central core to each archetype which has two aspects. One is oriented upward, toward the spiritual world; it is teleological in character, connected to destiny. The other aspect of the archetypal core is oriented downward, toward instinctual, biological processes; it is related to origin.

The garden can be considered as an expression of an archetype. It has the dynamism not only of the numinous, but also of the dual aspects of the archetypal core—one oriented toward the spiritual realm, the other toward the instinctual, biological processes.

There is a deep and abiding interest in gardens in much of Western culture. An ever-increasing number of magazines, clubs, shows, books and lectures are devoted to the subject. In my own back yard, the Garden Club of Toronto has an annual spring flower show attended by more and more people each year. Since 1998 it has been held in a gigantic convention center, a space so huge that the stamina of an Olympic athlete is needed to walk through all the displays.

What do so many people seek to find at such an event? Well, in Canada, when we see a plant flourishing at the end of a long winter, there is an undeniable sense of being in the presence of a miracle. Behold! The unknowable life force has created this unique beauty. Each plant is a vision. I think of the Dark Woman of my dream saying, "It's my party!" In the presence of abundant spring blossoms we witness the light of the divine in matter. We are participating in a mystery of holy immanence and transcendence—spirit and matter united.

Our response to gardens may be an attempt to balance the power of the industrial and technological developments of the past two centuries. I see the psychic situation in which we are now living in Western civilization depicted in the picture entitled *The Scream* by Edward Munch. The anguished outcry, the scream, of our time is that the transcendent spirit cannot be heard anymore. Western culture assumes to know it all. This becomes not only a psychological problem, but also a religious one. Too much weight is given to human knowledge, will and action. Impressive as these can be, they can also create more problems than they solve. There is a radical detachment from the psychic soil of the instincts and the ancestors which causes great suffering.

Figure 11. *The Scream* (1895), lithograph by Edward Munch.

Our psychic ground has to be renewed, but this can only happen if the unconscious has a chance to enter, to participate in life. If there is too much agony, as in *The Scream*, it is almost impossible for renewal to find a place to root. The warmth of the animal and vegetative kingdoms of the earth is missing. Healing of the one-sidedness comes from the depths of nature with its rhythms and cycles, and its paradox of order and chaos. The right attitude is also needed: the patience to wait for the new development to emerge and the willingness to serve it.

The miraculous abundance of a well-tended garden is a welcome antidote to the mechanical mode dominating contemporary life. Sometimes, when engulfed in the hectic pace of city life, I find myself contemplating this image: each of us is like a plant, ultimately rooted in the divine garden of life. Then the words of Jesus, as a symbol of the Self, remind me of our psychic structure: "I am the vine, you are the branches. Those who abide in me and I in them bear much fruit, because apart from me you can do nothing." (John 15:5)

Origin and Destiny

The garden as a place of origin as well as destiny is deeply rooted in the Judeo-Christian tradition. Linked to the mysterious beginning and end of human life, it is connected to the unfathomable central fire, the essence of existence. Thus the symbol of the primordial garden radiates numinosity, while at the same time it is a structuring principle.

In the Biblical account of creation, the original chaos was ordered first by the separation of light from darkness, above from below, water from land. Then on the third day God said, "Let the earth put forth vegetables: plants yielding seed, and fruit trees of every kind." (Gen. 1:11) Later, on the sixth day, man and woman were created. God orients them to the world by saying,

> See, I have given you every plant yielding seed that is upon the face of all the earth, and every tree with seed in its fruit; you shall have them for food. And to every beast of the earth, and to every bird of the air, and to everything that creeps on the earth, everything that has the breath of life, I have given every green plant for food. (Gen. 1:29-30; New Revised Standard Version)

The Lord God is represented as the primal gardener. The garden, the nurturing mother to all creation, is the beginning of life as well as the means by which it is sustained. Thus the garden itself is ancestor to all life on the planet. It is a living, female principle responding to the breath of the creator God that blew over the face of the waters.

In the second creation story given in Genesis, the Garden of Eden was created. It was the responsibility and destiny of the newly formed human beings to care for it:

> In the day that the Lord God made the earth and the heavens, when no plant of the field was yet in the earth and no herb of the field had yet sprung up—for the Lord God had not caused it to rain upon the earth, and there was no one to till the ground . . . then the Lord God formed man from the dust of the ground and breathed into his nostrils the breath of life; and the man became a living being. And the Lord God planted a garden in Eden, in the east; and there he put the man whom he had formed. (Gen. 2:4-5, 7-8)

> The Lord God took the man and put him in the garden to till it and keep it. (Gen. 2:15).

> Then the Lord God said, "It is not good that man should be alone; I will make him a helper as his partner." (Gen. 2:18).

After the first man and woman ate the forbidden fruit of the tree of knowledge of good and evil,

> They heard the sound of the Lord God walking in the garden at the time of the evening breeze, and the man and his wife hid themselves from the presence of the Lord God among the trees of the garden. (Gen. 3:8).

Various punishments were meted out for their violation. Then, for fear that they might also eat from the tree of life, thereby becoming immortal, "the Lord God sent him forth from the garden of Eden, to till the ground." (Gen. 3:23) They were driven out, and "at the east of the garden of Eden" the Lord God "placed the cherubim, and a sword flaming and turning to guard the way to the tree of life." (Gen. 3:24)

Thus the garden is the place for an encounter between humanity and divinity. Joseph Campbell notes:

> The Garden of Eden is a metaphor for that innocence that is innocent of time, innocent of opposites, and that is the prime center out of which consciousness then becomes aware of the changes.[206]

---

[206] *The Power of Myth,* p. 59.

Figure 12. The Garden of Eden watered by four rivers.
(Byzantine painting, 12th century)

After their disobedience, Adam and Eve were exiled from the garden, which is guarded by fire to protect the tree of life. The conscious life of humanity began here. East of Eden, human beings are responsible for tilling the ground.

Not only does the relationship to the garden affect earthly life, it also influences the destiny of the soul in the hereafter. The Biblical vision of the New Jerusalem, recorded in the Book of Revelation, illustrates this. When the soul finds its way to Paradise, it sees a heavenly version of the garden of Eden:

> The angel showed me the river of the water of life, bright as crystal, flowing from the throne of God and of the Lamb, through the middle of the street of the city. On either side of the river is the tree of life with its twelve kinds of fruits, producing its fruits each month; and the leaves of the tree are for the healing of the nations. (Rev. 22:1-2)

Clearly the garden has a central place in the Judeo-Christian tradition concerning the origins and purpose of life, as well as the process of living. In the garden there is an intermingling of the divine with the human. At times, the divine is experienced as immanent, dwelling within the universe of the garden. At other times it seems transcendent, beyond the boundaries of human, earthly life. Thus the garden's dual aspects—spiritual and biological—are part and parcel of the symbolic expression characteristic of an archetype.

Gardens in the Highlands of Papua New Guinea

Another of the defining moments in my relationship with the symbol of the garden came when I attended a series of lectures on the Highlands of Papua New Guinea, given by the anthropologist Dr. Paul Roche in Toronto. It was exciting to discover the central role of the gardens in that culture. In their practices and attitudes to gardens, I could see many features that have implications for the analytic process. I also saw many of the themes that emerged in the story of *The Secret Garden*.

Source of food

The main function of gardens in the Highlands of Papua New Guinea is to provide the staple crop of sweet potatoes which sustains the family and clan. The cultivation of the gardens is mainly the responsibility of the women. Men participate by guarding the area, repairing fences and doing the heavy lifting. In *The Secret Garden*, it is Mary's ingenuity and imagination that is responsible for waking up the garden. It is her project, to which Dickon, like his male counterparts in Papua New Guinea, gives support. In the gardening work of analysis, nurturing and feminine relatedness to cycles are helpful qualities.

Privacy for conjugal relations

A second function of the Papua New Guinea garden is to provide a private place where husband and wife can have sexual relations, since they do not live together. Men live together communally after they have been initiated into manhood. Women live in their own dwellings with the children. The garden offers husband and wife some necessary privacy. As well, having sexual relations in the garden is thought to increase the fertility of the garden. Thus it provides a temenos for a *coniunctio* with man, woman and nature.

Figure 13. Garden in the Highlands of Papua New Guinea.

While this is not common practice in Western culture, there are many similar instances. The imagery of erotic life occurring in nature is provocative on an imaginative and symbolic level. A Biblical example is found in the Song of Solomon (also called the Canticle of Canticles). Here the garden is depicted as the place where the lovers meet, as well as being a metaphor for the beloved. The lovers are thought to be King Solomon and a Shulamite shepherdess who are engaged in a rhapsodic love duet.[207]

Each invites the other to meet in the garden, which is described in luxurious detail. The imagery of the garden is also used to describe their love. The poems express the joy the lovers experience. They have also been interpreted as a description of the love of God for his people.[208] The lover, describing his beloved, says,

> A garden inclosed is my sister, *my* spouse; a spring shut up, a fountain sealed. Thy plants *are* an orchard of pomegranates, with pleasant fruits: . . . a fountain of gardens, a well of living waters. (Song of Sol. 4:12-13, 15; Authorized King James Version)

The maiden responds,

> Awake, O north wind; and come, thou south; blow upon my garden, *that* the spices thereof may flow out. Let my beloved come into his garden, and eat his pleasant fruits. (Song of Sol. 4:16; Authorized King James Version)

The lover accepts her invitation:

> I am come into my garden, my sister, *my* spouse. (Song of Sol. 5:1; Authorized King James Version)

An example of the garden as a setting for erotic, sexual encounters in twentieth-century literature is *Lady Chatterley's Lover* by D.H. Lawrence. The passion between Lady Chatterley and her lover, Mellors, the gardener, could not be expressed in the stifling atmosphere of the lord's manor. Their Eros, kindled in the garden, could only be lived close to

---

[207] See Roland Murphy, "Canticle of Canticles," in *Jerome Biblical Commentary,* pp. 506ff.

[208] Ibid., p. 507.

nature, in Mellors' hut. The transformative intensity of the experience, evident in the following passage, was releasing:

> He took her in his arms again and drew her to him, . . . It was gone, the resistance was gone, and she began to melt in a marvellous peace. . . . And she felt him like a flame of desire, yet tender, and she felt herself melting in the flame. . . . And it seemed she was like the sea, nothing but dark waves rising and heaving, heaving with a great swell, so that slowly her whole darkness was in motion. . . . she was deeper and deeper and deeper disclosed, and heavier the billows of her rolled away to some shore, uncovering her. . . . She was gone, she was not, and she was born: a woman.[209]

In the ancient world Eros was considered to be a god with healing qualities. Von Franz outlines how this was viewed and the possible underlying psychological reasons:

> At the entrance of the Aesculapian temple in Epidaurus, when the sick came to be healed of psychological or physical diseases, were the pictures of the two healing principles of Eros and Methe (drunkenness). Love and drunkenness are the great healing forces for the soul and body. The drunkenness referred to here is not that obtained through alcohol. . . . This experience of elevation and of eternity links us again with the archetypal basis of the psyche and has a healing and transforming effect.[210]

Eros, one of the healing gods in ancient Greece, is also the "divine child" in some mystery cults.[211]

In one of my own dreams I experienced the gift of Eros in a forest garden that imparted a feeling of blissful healing:

> I had a very free erotic encounter with a young black man. We were quite uninhibited. It was a delightful encounter. He had some special ointment, which smelled and tasted like apples, that he tenderly applied to my skin.
>
> Later we went swimming in a deep pool in the midst of some rocks. It was fed by a river. There were other people present, creating a playful at-

---

[209] *Lady Chatterley's Lover*, pp. 173f.

[210] *Golden Ass*, pp. 83f.

[211] Ibid., p. 84.

mosphere. But they were all strangers to me.

Then we were walking in a forest. It was extraordinary. The soil was very dark, rich, and fertile. There was a lot of decay and rebirth in evidence. I became aware of this process going on all around as we walked in the forest. I marveled in particular at a small garden. There were some white birch logs that had decayed in the center, creating rich soil where flowers were blooming. The logs were now containers—like planters—for the flowers.

There was a special hush or silence everywhere. I had a sense of awe, a feeling that I was seeing something special, even holy. I was not aware of anyone else in the forest now, but I did not feel alone. Everything was filled with an almost tangibly vibrant vitality which was part of a living process. Somehow I was witnessing that process. It made me feel calm and free.

Home of ancestral spirits

The gardens in the Highlands of Papua New Guinea not only provide food and privacy for sexual relations. They have another vital function. They are considered to be inhabited by the spirits of the ancestors as well as the nature spirits belonging to the land itself. The connection between humans and these spirits must always be safeguarded. It is not to be taken for granted. Therefore the garden is regarded as a sacred place. In our own culture, cemeteries are usually carefully landscaped, garden-like areas, where we behave with respectful quietude.

In our story, it seems that Lilias Craven in her afterlife existence dwells in the secret garden. Often in the garden of analysis one discovers how alive are deceased friends and relatives in the depths of the psyche.

Magic rituals

Rituals of magic are used in the Highlands of Papua New Guinea to propitiate the ancestors and nature spirits so that they will encourage growth. What are the principles on which these rituals are based?

James George Frazer explores this in his influential work of social anthropology, *The Golden Bough*. He considers that there are two main principles:

First, that like produces like, or that an effect resembles its cause; and second, that things which have once been in contact with each other continue to act on each other at a distance after the physical contact has been severed. The former principle may be called the Law of Similarity, the latter the Law of Contact or Contagion.[212]

According to the Law of Similarity, a person may produce the desired effect by imitating it. According to the Law of Contagion, an object (or person) will acquire the properties of whatever it has been in contact with. In practical terms these two forms of magic are used actively by the individuals cultivating the gardens. By using contagious magic the nature spirits are invoked to act favorably with respect to the new crops. Imitative magic, based upon the Law of Similarity, is used in the casting of spells over the crops so that they will imitate the abundance of the surrounding nature.[213]

In our story, the children felt the secret garden to be full of magic, which they considered to be the source of all the miracles they experienced. They are healed by being in contact with the new growth (contagious magic) as well as by aligning themselves with the processes they witness there (imitative magic). This was an important part of their imaginative response to the garden. Recall that Mary was a great believer in magic:

Secretly she quite believed that Dickon worked Magic, . . . on everything near him and that was why people liked him so much and wild creatures knew he was their friend.

Colin, thrilled by the garden, declares, "I'm going to see everything grow here. I'm going to grow here myself." He saw it all, watching each change as it took place. "Every morning he was brought out and every hour of each day when it didn't rain he spent in the garden." As he watched the new growth he reflected,

Something began pushing things out of the soil and making things out of

---

[212] *The Golden Bough: A Study of Magic and Religion,* p. 14.

[213] See R.F. Fortune, *Sorcerers of Dobu: The Social Anthropology of the Dobu Islanders of the Western Pacific*, p. 125.

nothing. One day things weren't there and another they were. . . . I keep saying to myself, "What is it? What is it? It's something. It can't be nothing! I don't know its name so I call it Magic."

These attitudes parallel the traditional Papua New Guinea belief in imitative and contagious magic. Healing and renewal in *The Secret Garden* occur by being in the presence of the "magic" within its precinct.

What might these phenomena mean symbolically? What relationship might they have to analytical psychology? The spirits of nature and the ancestors could be viewed as the whole instinctual and archetypal world of symbols encountered throughout the analytical process, as one cultivates the garden of the soul. The invocation of magic in the garden suggests the activation of the transcendent function with its potential for healing.

Imitative magic is based on the principle that like produces like. In analytical psychology there is an understanding that the meaning of an illness may be closely connected with its cure. This is reminiscent of the ancient oracle of Apollo: "The wounder heals."[214] Contagious magic, on the other hand, is based on the principle: once in contact, always in contact. Contact with the transcendent function is healing.

The principle of reciprocity

In addition to magic, there are other principles governing the cultivation of the gardens in Papua New Guinea. The principle of reciprocity structures life. It means that a balance must be kept at all times. Planting and harvesting are a continuous process. When a plant is mature, it is harvested and a new seedling planted in its place. The rule is that a person may harvest only what she has planted. All cultivation in the gardens requires careful consideration and respect in order for the plants to flourish. The garden is considered a living place where the staple crop of sweet potatoes grow. They are regarded as living beings which require politeness and care in order to thrive.

The garden must never be exploited. This means that a person cannot

---

[214] C.A. Meier, *Healing Dream and Ritual: Ancient Incubation and Modern Psychotherapy*, p. 134.

just take from it but must always be mindful of the principle of reciprocity, of balance, and give the garden nourishment. It is understood that this is necessary because if one part of the system is abused or destroyed, the whole is affected.

By this careful approach, space is created for the nurturing of human life in the face of huge forces of uncertainty. The garden is generally located on the edge of the wild, just as the forest adjoined my grandparents' garden. The task of the gardener is to support those elements that can work favorably, to appease those elements which might be destructive, and not to take anything by force or theft.

A similar principle functions in relation to working with the unconscious: one cannot just take from the unconscious without a fair exchange. Devotion and respect from the ego are required in order for the unconscious to yield its harvest in its own time.

This principle of reciprocity, the maintaining of a constant balance between giving and taking, is apparent in Dickon's caring relatedness to the natural world. He lives with an attitude of reciprocity toward the world. He explains to Mary that "a body 'as to move gentle an' speak low when wild things is about." His knowledge comes from his sympathetic, engaged interest in the living beings around him, not from an urge for exploitation. Mary and Colin learn and develop by being in contact with Dickon.

Fallow periods

Another principle governing the cultivation of gardens in Papua New Guinea is the necessity for fallow periods. After a section of the garden has yielded several harvests it is allowed to revert to bush in order to regain its fertility. When this bush develops sufficiently it provides lumber to maintain the structure of the garden (its fences), houses and boats. Eventually this bush will be prepared once again to become a garden. Certainly the secret garden, abandoned and locked, experienced a long fallow period, almost reverting to bush, before Mary discovered it.

This is important from a psychological point of view. Sometimes, when a person enters a fallow period in life, there is a tendency to be discouraged because nothing seems to be happening. The image of land lying fallow for an interval is instructive. The bias toward goal-oriented activity does at times need to be superseded by a period of relative dormancy because of its potential for renewal.

Pondering this condition, Clarissa Pinkola Estes asks, "What is this faithful process of spirit and seed that touches empty ground and makes it rich again?"—

> Whatever we set our days to might be the least of what we do, if we do not understand that something is waiting for us to make ground for it, something that lingers near us, something that loves, something that waits for the right ground to be made so it can make its full presence known.
>
> I am certain that as we stand in care of this faithful force, that what has seemed dead is dead no longer, what has seemed lost, is no longer lost, that which some have claimed impossible, is made clearly possible, and what ground is fallow is only resting—resting and waiting for the blessed seed to arrive on the wind "with all God speed."[215]

Jung considers the seeds of future conscious developments to be in the unconscious, which is the container for everything:

> The unconscious contains all those psychic components that have fallen below the threshold, as well as subliminal sense perceptions. Moreover, we know, from abundant experience as well as for theoretical reasons, that besides this the unconscious contains all the material that has *not yet* reached the threshold of consciousness. These are the seeds of future conscious contents. Equally we have every reason to suppose that the unconscious is never quiescent in the sense of being inactive, but presumably is ceaselessly engaged in the grouping and regrouping of so-called unconscious fantasies.[216]

Elsewhere Jung similarly describes the unconscious as a container for psychic processes related to past, present and future:

> Although the unconscious is a receptacle for everything that is forgotten, past, and repressed, it is also the sphere in which all subliminal processes take place. It contains sense-perceptions that are still too weak to reach

---

[215] *The Faithful Gardener: A Wise Tale About That Which Can Never Die*, pp. 74f.
[216] *Two Essays*, CW 7, par. 445.

consciousness, and, furthermore, is the matrix out of which the whole psychic future grows.[217]

During a psychologically fallow period it may be possible for the seeds in the unconscious to be sufficiently nourished to sprout and become visible to the ego. Jung recognizes the importance of such intervals in life. He writes about this in his commentary on "The Secret of the Golden Flower":

> The art of letting things happen, action through non-action, letting go of oneself as taught by Meister Eckhart, became for me the key that opens the door to the way. We must be able to let things happen in the psyche. For us, this is an art of which most people know nothing. Consciousness is forever interfering, helping, correcting, and negating, never leaving the psychic processes to grow in peace.[218]

Jesus too speaks of the fallow period. Although it may seem like death, it is actually a precursor to new life:

> Verily, I tell you, unless a grain of wheat falls into the earth, and dies, it remains just a single grain; but if it dies, it bears much fruit. (John 12:24)

Here again the duality of nature is apparent. Not all seeds become fruitful. This reality is described in the Biblical parable of the sower:

> A sower went out to sow his seed. And as he sowed, some seed fell along the footpath, where it was trampled on, and the birds ate it up. Some seed fell on rock and, after coming up, withered for lack of moisture. Some seed fell in among thistles, and the thistles grew up and choked it. And some of the seed fell into good soil, and grew, and yielded a hundredfold. (Luke 8:5-8)

Ritual sacrifice

A final principle observed for the sake of enriching the gardens in Papua New Guinea is honoring of the ancestors and the nature spirits by the ritual sacrifice of pigs. This is another example of reciprocity: since

---

[217] "Analytical Psychology and 'Weltanschauung,' " *The Structure and Dynamics of the Psyche,* CW 8, par. 709.

[218] *Alchemical Studies,* CW 13, par. 20.

the pigs grew by eating sweet potatoes, it is fitting that they be sacrificed in the garden so that their blood can fertilize the soil. This is thought to create a propitious environment for a new crop because not only does it enrich the ground, it is also done for the sake of the ancestors whose spirits live in the gardens and appreciate this attention.

In addition, this sacrifice constitutes an important festival. It is an occasion for feasting and social renewal both within the clan and with neighboring clans. Thus sacrifice and renewal are part of the same cycle.

In *The Secret Garden,* though the death of Lilias Craven, Colin's mother, was not a willing sacrifice, it was the beginning of a long process of renewal. Her presence was felt in the garden. Dickon says that his mother thinks that Mrs. Craven has often been around Misselthwaite Manor, "many a time lookin' after Master Colin, same as all mothers do when they're took out o' th' world. They have to come back, tha' sees." He even goes so far as to say that it was Mrs. Craven (in her afterlife existence) that set them to work in the garden and gave them the inspiration to include Colin.

When an individual faces the necessity of sacrifice, it is not usually a cause for celebration. Sometimes one sacrifices spontaneity and vitality for the sake of duty. This can lead to psychological stagnation. There is also the kind of sacrifice that, in spite of suffering, is the beginning of renewal. Analysis itself can be felt as a sacrifice in terms of the time, money and effort involved. But to continue in one's habitual patterns of adaptation may become a torment. Life may bring a person to a crucial impasse of profound loneliness and depression, as well as an impassioned wish that it were not so. This state then becomes the impetus for a deeper process of self-discovery. Painful as this may be, to stay in the nadir of the impasse is worse.

In the face of the uncertain outcome of a sacrifice, a person may rigidly hold on to habitual patterns in order to ward off terror. The ego tries to keep new energy out of consciousness in an effort to cling to what is familiar. This attachment prevents one from living congruently with the deeper, unique reality of his or her own individuality. Something that wants to be incorporated into the person's life is excluded. Sacrifice, which is a form of death, may be necessary in order to move again into life. Here death and life are like partners. If there is no capacity to sacrifice the old ways, the new life cannot develop.

To surrender sterile ways of living in order for a new orientation to develop is not a task the ego can accomplish alone. The deeper resources of the psyche are needed. Just as in the gardens in the Highlands of Papua New Guinea, we must call up the experience of Eros, reciprocity, fallow periods, magic (the transcendent function) and sacrifice.

While imagining ourselves as gardeners of the psyche, we must acknowledge another reality: we are also the gardens that are being cultivated. In Jesus' words:

> Do you not say, "Four months more, then comes the harvest?" But I tell you, look around you, and see how the fields are ripe for harvesting. The reaper is already receiving wages and is gathering fruit for eternal life, so that sower and reaper may rejoice together. (John 4:35-6)

Implications for Analytical Psychology

In analytical psychology, it is contact with the archetypal world through symbols that brings healing, or balance, or the capacity to endure suffering. The reason for this is the nature of the psyche itself. Jung believed that the human psyche has an inherently spiritual function and that no person in the second half of life could find healing without having a relationship to that aspect of the psyche:

> Among all my patients in the second half of life—that is to say, over thirty-five—there has not been one whose problem in the last resort was not that of finding a religious outlook on life. It is safe to say that every one of them fell ill because he had lost what the living religions of every age have given to their followers, and none of them has been really healed who did not regain his religious outlook.[219]

---

[219] "Psychotherapists or the Clergy," *Psychology and Religion,* CW 11, par. 509. (Jung was not referring to belief in a particular creed or membership in a church, but rather to a certain attitude of mind, which he described in terms of the Latin *religio,* meaning "a careful consideration and observation of certain dynamic factors that are conceived as 'powers': spirits, daemons, gods, laws, ideas, ideals, or whatever . . . [that one] has found powerful, dangerous, or helpful."—"Psychology and Religion," ibid., par. 8.)

This spiritual dimension is related to the affinity of the psyche for symbols, which is often ignored in our rationalistic culture. Jung termed our symbol-making capacity the transcendent function. This idea was introduced earlier, but I think it deserves further elaboration here.

The transcendent function

The transcendent function is a mysterious, even magical, psychic faculty activated, at least in part, by the tension which arises between consciousness and the unconscious. It is facilitated by an ego which can maintain its standpoint while becoming aware of the unconscious through material offered in dreams, fantasies and active imagination. This could be compared to the process of gardening: tilling the ground, planting the seeds, watering the new shoots, then letting nature take its course. Jung describes it:

> The process of coming to terms with the unconscious is a true labour, a work which involves both action and suffering. It has been named the "transcendent function" because it represents a function based on real and "imaginary," or rational and irrational, data, thus bridging the yawning gulf between conscious and unconscious.[220]

He points out that this is not a forced or mechanical effort but rather a natural process. However, it does require the capacity to hold the tension in a conflict situation. He continues,

> It is a natural process, a manifestation of the energy that springs from the tension of opposites, and it consists in a series of fantasy-occurrences which appear spontaneously in dreams and visions.[221]

This capacity is vital for psychological growth because it opens a person to previously unseen perspectives in both feeling and attitude, with the result that there are new possibilities for life. Von Franz explains:

> It is "transcendent," for not only does it transcend our conscious grasp, but it is the only thing which, through the help of a symbol, enables man to

---

[220] *Two Essays,* CW 7, par. 121.
[221] Ibid.

pass from one psychic state to another. . . . We would be forever stuck in an acquired state of consciousness if this transcendent function of the psyche did not help us over into new attitudes by creating a symbol which shares in both worlds: being associated with the psychic state of the present as well as the future, the symbol helps us over.[222]

She points out that this process requires a certain amount of devotion and Eros in order to be effective:

The transcendent function requires a minimum of conscious libido. The healing function of the unconscious cannot bring us over "to the other shore" if we do not give it libido, that means conscious attention.[223]

And she goes on to say that if a person fails to give this attention there can be serious consequences:

One sees this so tragically in people who have dragged on for perhaps twenty years under terrific hidden suffering from a neurotic symptom. Such people have been arrested at the shore for lack of money for Charon. They did not have the right instruction, or they lacked the instinct or the generosity to follow it.[224]

Thus a person's attitude is an important factor in the process of psychological gardening and development.

*

To sum up: the garden is a sacred place in Papua New Guinea. While it is clearly designated as separate from where people live, it is central to life both on a physical and spiritual level. It provides food and privacy for sexual relations. It is the sacred space for the sacrifice which keeps a balance with the ancestors and the nature spirits. This is an occasion for celebration and renewal. The principle of reciprocity governs. The people are constantly in relationship with the processes of the garden; it is a whole system with no division between the inner and outer worlds.

In contrast, there is separation between these two realms in the West.

---

[222] *Golden Ass*, p. 127.
[223] Ibid., p. 128.
[224] Ibid.

Human beings were banished from the Garden of Eden. Furthermore, technology and industrialization have severed us from an organic connection to nature. Thus we are cut adrift from our roots.

Where is the sacred place in which we might reestablish a living relationship with the psychic soil? How can we enter into a conscious relationship with the unconscious? Where is the stillness for Eros and the transcendent capacity within the psyche to put forth its green shoots? Both Jung and von Franz recognize the need for this. She recalls Jung's views:

> As Jung repeatedly pointed out, modern human beings are already so heavily overloaded, both internally and externally, with precepts, demands, advice, slogans, collective suggestions, idealism, and other (also good) guidelines, that it is perhaps worth the effort to provide them with an opportunity to realize their own nature in an unforced and fully self-responsible fashion.[225]

The effect of this is a deeper appreciation of the divine essence of life which is a source of strength. Von Franz observes:

> This is the way, perhaps, that the divine influence makes its appearance in the psyche in its purest form—all by itself. And it is also likely that the individual best resists the destructive collective influences of his time when, all alone and through his own inner experience, he becomes rooted in his relationship to God.[226]

---

[225] "Active Imagination in the Psychology of C.G. Jung," in *Psychotherapy*, pp. 161f.
[226] Ibid., p. 162.

7
Intimations of Eternity

Ultimately the secret garden, like all symbols, points to the ineffable, unknowable realms beyond human comprehension. It has intimations of eternity. Just as human life is represented in Genesis as beginning in the garden, it also seems to be our destiny after death. In the story, Lilias appears to her husband, Archie Craven, in a dream that "was so real he did not feel as if he were dreaming." When he asked her, "Lilias, where are you?" she replied, "In the garden!" Her answer "was like a sound from a golden flute." The garden is the dwelling place for her soul.

The affinity of the soul with the garden is apparent in spiritual and psychological life. Vegetation imagery represents the psychic mystery of life, as well as death and resurrection. This can be seen in depictions of the ancient Egyptian beliefs concerning the afterlife as well as in the dreams of contemporary individuals who are approaching death. The Gospel of John also uses this imagery to indicate the psychic process of death as a precursor to new life:

> In truth, in very truth I tell you, a grain of wheat remains a solitary grain
> unless it falls into the ground and dies; but if it dies, it bears a rich harvest.
> (John 12:24; New English Bible)

This is reflected in Jung's understanding, noted earlier, that human life is "like a plant that lives on its rhizome."[227]

The passage from life to death is part of the eternal flux. An important function of dreams is preparation for new thresholds in a person's journey, one of which is death, an aspect of individuation. This point is discussed by Emmanuel Kennedy-Xipolitas in the foreword to Marie-Louise von Franz's book, *On Dreams and Death*:

> Individuation—the process of psychic and spiritual growth—is actually a
> preparation for death, the most essential transformation of our whole be-

---

[227] *Memories, Dreams, Reflections*, p. 4.

ing. . . . then it would seem that individuation is the essence of life's deeper meaning. . . . Self-knowledge means at the same time a reunion of the soul with God. . . . *This* is individuation or Self-realization.[228]

There are examples from Jung's critical illness and approaching death of dream-visions containing symbols of the garden and vegetation which illustrate the individuation process as he passed from earthly life back to the rhizome. When he was critically ill, he had a vision of the heavenly garden of pomegranates. He described it as "purest bliss."[229] The vision included the sacred marriage which gave him "ineffable states of joy."[230] He said that the visions and experiences were utterly real; there was nothing subjective about them, and they all had the quality of absolute objectivity.

Although such an experience can scarcely be understood, its effect can reverberate for the rest of one's earthly life. This was so for Jung, who wrote: "It is impossible to convey the beauty and intensity of emotion during these visions. They are the most tremendous things I have ever experienced."[231]

Here is Jung's vision of the sacred marriage in the garden of the pomegranates:

Everything around me seemed enchanted. . . . I myself was, so it seemed, in the Pardes Rimmonim, the garden of the pomegranates, and the wedding of Tifereth with Malchuth was taking place. Or else I was Rabbi Simon ben Jochai, whose wedding in the afterlife was being celebrated. It was the mystic marriage as it appears in the Cabbalistic tradition. I cannot tell you how wonderful it was. I could only think continually, "Now this is the garden of pomegranates! Now this is the marriage of Malchuth with Tifereth!" I do not know exactly what part I played in it. At bottom it was I myself: I was the marriage. And my beatitude was that of a blissful wedding.[232]

---

[228] *On Dreams and Death*, p. xi.
[229] *Memories, Dreams, Reflections*, p. 294.
[230] Ibid.
[231] Ibid., p. 295.
[232] Ibid., p. 294.

The spiritual aspect of this wedding then became more explicit:

> Gradually the garden of the pomegranates faded away and changed. There
> followed the Marriage of the Lamb, in a Jerusalem festively bedecked. I
> cannot describe what it was like in detail. These were ineffable states of
> joy. Angels were present, and light. I myself was the "Marriage of the
> Lamb."[233]

This is reminiscent of the scene of marriage described in Revelation:

> Then I heard what seemed to be the voice of a great multitude, like the
> sound of many waters and like the sound of mighty thunderpeals crying
> out, "Hallelujah! For the Lord our God the Almighty reigns. Let us rejoice
> and exult and give him the glory for the marriage of the Lamb has come,
> and his bride has made herself ready." (Rev. 19:6-7)

When that vision fades, the next one appears. In it Jung sees a cosmic,
sacred marriage in an amphitheater at the end of a green valley:

> I walked up a wide valley to the end, where a gentle chain of hills began.
> The valley ended in a classical amphitheater. It was magnificently situated
> in a green landscape. And there, in this theater, the *hierosgamos* was being
> celebrated. Men and women dancers came onstage, and upon a flower-
> decked couch All-Father Zeus and Hera consummated the mystic mar-
> riage, as it is described in *The Iliad*.[234]

Jung reflects upon the experience of these visions as giving him a
sense of being interwoven in a totality beyond temporal life:

> We shy away from the word "eternal," but I can describe the experience
> only as the ecstasy of a non-temporal state in which present, past, and fu-
> ture are one. Everything that happens in time had been brought together
> into a concrete whole. Nothing was distributed over time, nothing could be
> measured by temporal concepts. The experience might best be defined as a
> state of feeling, but one which cannot be produced by the imagination. . . .
> One is interwoven into an indescribable whole and yet observes it with
> complete objectivity.[235]

---

[233] Ibid.

[234] Ibid.

[235] Ibid., pp. 295f.

Jung recovered from that grave illness to continue living for another seventeen years. As a result of these visions he always lived with the perception that there was a realm of existence beyond the earthly plane. He says,

> Although my belief in the world returned to me, I have never since entirely freed myself of the impression that this life is a segment of existence which is enacted in a three-dimensional boxlike universe especially set up for it.[236]

Shortly after his eighty-fifth birthday on July 26, 1960, Jung became seriously ill again. He had been at his Tower in Bollingen for the occasion, then went to the west of Switzerland for a short holiday where he fell ill. This necessitated his return home to Küsnacht where he had the following dream:

> He saw the "other Bollingen" bathed in a glow of light, and a voice told him that it was now completed and ready for habitation. Then far below he saw a mother wolverine teaching her child to dive and swim in a stretch of water.[237]

In the next world, the hallowed, liminal space of Bollingen, his country home, was apparently ready to receive his soul. Barbara Hannah comments on the significance of this dream:

> This was obviously a death dream, for he had often dreamed of this "other Bollingen" before, in various stages of construction, and he had always spoken of it as being in the unconscious, in the Beyond. The end of the dream had the same meaning: the dreamer must soon pass into another element (usually called another world) and learn as different a way of adaptation as the young wolverine, who was already at home on dry ground, had to learn in the water. Evidently Mother Nature was ready for the change and prepared to give him her full support.[238]

The image of the "other Bollingen" can be understood as representing the "house not made by human hands" described by the apostle Paul:

---

[236] Ibid., p. 295.

[237] Barbara Hannah, *Jung: His Life and Work*, p. 344.

[238] Ibid.

> For we know that if the earthly frame that houses us today should be de-
> molished, we possess a building which God has provided—a house not
> made by human hands, eternal and in heaven. (2 Cor. 5:1; New English
> Bible)

Jung died on June 6, 1961. His last dreams, recorded a few days before his death, contain moving imagery of a completed individuation
process and of being received as an individual by the roots of the tree of
life, or by what Jung called "the rhizome." Here are the dreams as recounted by Barbara Hannah:

> 1) He saw a big, round block of stone in a high bare place and on it was
> inscribed: "This shall be a sign unto you of wholeness and oneness."
>
> 2) A lot of vessels, pottery vases, on the right side of a square place.
>
> 3) A square of trees, all fibrous roots, coming up from the ground and sur-
> rounding him. There were gold threads gleaming among the roots.[239]

The symbol of the walled garden also points beyond itself toward the
unknown realms. A woman in analysis with von Franz had the following
haunting dream the night after Jung's death, of which she was unaware at
the time. She did not know him personally. Here is the dream as it is related by von Franz:

> She was at a garden party where many people were standing around on a
> lawn. Jung was among them. He was wearing a strange outfit: in front his
> jacket and trousers were bright green, in the back they were black. Then
> she saw a black wall which had a hole cut out of it in exactly the same
> shape as Jung's stature. Jung suddenly stepped into this hole, and now all
> that one could see was a complete black surface, although everyone knew
> that he was still there. Then the dreamer looked at herself and discovered
> that she, too, was wearing such clothes, green in front and black be-
> hind.[240]

The contemporary Swiss mystic, Joa Bolendas, recounts her visions in
the book *So That You May Be One*. In one of them she sees a series of

---

[239] Ibid., p. 347.

[240] *On Dreams and Death*, p. 155.

walled gardens, all linked to each other. Darkness prevails outside the walls. She understands these gardens as faith. But this faith is not a rationalist attitude of the conscious mind. Rather, it is the outcome of an experience of primal light. As the translator, John Hill, explains in the foreword to the book:

> Primal light, according to the Johannine teachings in Joa's texts, approximates to the transcendental and metaphysical light of the mystics; it is an expression of the very light of God and all of creation, including the darkness of night.[241]

Here is a portion of her vision of the walled gardens:

> As I sat in the church, I saw a magnificent flower garden, full of the most beautiful flowers. Some single poppies, large and magnificent, were particularly noticeable. They were red and yellow in colour. Around this garden was a very ancient wall made of square stone. Something unseen raised me upward from the garden where I was standing. I saw other gardens with old stone walls joining them in places. All the gardens were linked to each other. And outside these gardens was darkness—dark night. . . . The flowers are the faithful—even the grass. . . . Every garden except one blossomed, and often a seed would be carried from one to another.[242]

While she saw these gardens as also being for each particular d enomination of faith, the metaphysical dimension referred to above is relevant for this consideration of the walled, secret garden as representing an experience of ultimate value on a personal as well as collective and possibly even cosmic level.

To the long-suffering protagonist in Solzhenitsyn's novel *Cancer Ward*, even the sight of a blossoming tree contained in a courtyard garden is a miraculous vision of hope and inspiration. Oleg Kostoglotov had just been discharged from the hospital after a long, difficult treatment for cancer. Facing an uncertain future, he hoped to find a miracle that day. He considered it to be "the first day of his new life."

---

[241] *So That You May Be One*, p. 40.
[242] Ibid., pp. 97f

As he embarked on this little additional piece of life, Oleg longed for it to be different from the main part he had lived through. He wished he could stop making mistakes now.[243]

He decided not to hurry so that he could notice every detail of this new day.

And then from the teahouse balcony he saw above the walled courtyard next door something pink and transparent. It looked like a puff dandelion, only it was six meters in diameter, a rosy, weightless balloon. He'd never seen anything so pink and so huge.

Could it be the apricot tree?

Oleg had learned a lesson. This was his reward for not hurrying. The lesson was—never rush on without looking around first.

He walked up to the railings and from on high gazed and gazed through this pink miracle.

It was his present to himself—his creation-day present.

It was like a fir tree decorated with candles in a room of a northern home. The flowering apricot was the only tree in this courtyard enclosed by clay walls and open only to the sky.[244]

Oleg gazed at the tree, breathing in its beauty.

The tree had buds like candles. When on the point of opening, the petals were pink in color, but once open they were pure white, like apple or cherry blossoms. The result was an incredible, tender pink. Oleg was trying to absorb it all into his eyes. He wanted to remember it for a long time.

He'd planned on finding a miracle, and he'd found one.

There were many joys in store for him today in this newly born world.[245]

*

From beginning to end the garden is both container and destination. It is a companion for the journey, feeding the hungry soul with the light of nature. I close with a memorable dream of my own. Since it occurred

---

[243] *Cancer Ward,* p. 489.

[244] Ibid.

[245] Ibid., p. 490.

near one of my birthdays, I think of it as *my* "creation-day present":

> I was walking with a man in a garden. We were inside some deep mystery. Something had opened up, so that we were inside and surrounded by it. Everything was very clear in the dream—that is, both the experience and the sense that I saw deeply and could understand. But when I woke up, I did not know what it was except perhaps it was the mystery of life it-self—though now I would have no idea how to describe what I seemed to see and know in the dream.

The mystery and magic of the secret garden is an abiding reality where temporal and eternal worlds unite. It is a temenos where the invisible plane underlying and supporting the visible one is manifest. It is also a place where one may find a deeper connection with what could be considered the womb of nature, the soul of the world.

Being present to the garden, one knows that, as Dylan Thomas says:

> The force that through the green fuse drives the flower
> Drives my green age.[246]

---

[246] "The Force that Through the Green Fuse Drives the Flower," in *Norton Anthology of Poetry*, pp. 713f.

Figure 14. Original woodcut by Mary Azarian, Vermont.

List of Illustrations and Credits

Bibliography

Adler, Gerhard. "Aspects of Jung's Personality." In *Psychological Perspectives*, vol. 6, no. 1 (Spring 1975).

Blakney, Raymond B., trans. *Meister Eckhart.* New York: Harper & Row, 1941.

Bolendas, Joa. *So That You May Be One.* Trans. John Hill. New York: Lindisfarne Books, 1997.

Brown, Schuyler. *Text and Psyche: Experiencing Scripture Today.* New York: Continuum, 1998.

Browning, Robert. *The Poetical Works of Robert Browning.* Ed. Robert Strange. Boston: Houghton Mifflin Co., 1974.

Burnett, Frances Hodgson. *The Secret Garden.* New York: HarperCollins, 1990.

Butala, Sharon. *The Perfection of the Morning: An Apprenticeship in Nature.* Toronto: HarperCollins, 1995.

Campbell, Joseph. *The Power of Myth.* Ed. Betty Sue Flowers. New York: Doubleday, 1991.

Concise Oxford Dictionary of Current English. London: Oxford University Press, 1964.

Cullman, Oscar. *Christ and Time: The Primitive Christian Conception of Time and History.* Trans. F.V. Filson. Philadelphia: The Westminster Press, 1964.

Dart, John, and Riegert, Ray, eds. *The Gospel of Thomas: Unearthing the Lost Words of Jesus.* Berkeley, CA: Seastone, 2000.

Dickens, Charles. *Great Expectations.* Toronto: Gage Educational Publishing Co., 1980.

Edinger, Edward F. *The Aion Lectures: Exploring the Self in C.G. Jung's* Aion. Ed. Deborah A. Wesley. Toronto: Inner City Books, 1996.

_____. *The Mysterium Lectures: A Journey through Jung's* Mysterium Coniunctionis. Toronto: Inner City Books, 1995.

Eliade, Mircea. *The Sacred and the Profane.* Trans. W.R. Trask. New York: Harcourt, Brace, Jovanovich, 1959.

Estes, Clarissa Pinkola. *The Faithful Gardener: A Wise Tale About That Which Can Never Die.* San Francisco: HarperCollins, 1995.

Fortune, R.F. *Sorcerers of Dobu. The Social Anthropology of the Dobu Island-ers of the Western Pacific.* New York: E.P. Dutton and Co., 1932.

Fox, Matthew, ed. *Hildegard of Bingen: Illuminations and Text.* Santa Fe, NM: Bear & Co., 1985.

Frazer, James George. *The Golden Bough: A Study of Magic and Religion.* Abridged Edition. New York: Macmillan, 1951.

Frye, Northrop. *The Double Vision: Language and Meaning in Religion.* To-ronto: University of Toronto Press, 1991.

Gebser, Jean. *The Ever-Present Origin.* Trans. Noel Barstad and Algis Micku-nas. Athens, OH: Ohio University Press, 1985.

Haas, Ernst. *The Creation.* New York: Penguin Books, 1976.

Hannah, Barbara. *Encounters with the Soul: Active Imagination as Developed by C.G. Jung.* Wilmette, IL: Chiron Publications, 2001.

_____. *Jung: His Life and Work. A Biographical Memoir.* Boston: Sham-bala, 1991.

_____. *Striving Towards Wholeness.* New York: G.P. Putnam's Sons, 1971.

Hillman, James. *Loose Ends: Primary Papers in Archetypal Psychology.* Irving, TX: Spring Publications, 1978.

Huizinga, Johan. *Homo Ludens. A Study of the Play Element in Culture.* Lon-don: Routledge & Kegan Paul, 1972.

Jackson, Graham. *The Secret Lore of Gardening: Patterns of Male Intimacy.* Toronto: Inner City Books, 1991.

Jacobi, Jolande. *Complex/Archetype/Symbol in the Psychology of C.G. Jung* (Bollingen Series LVII). Trans. Ralph Manheim. New York: Princeton Uni-versity Press, 1974.

Jaffe, Lawrence W. "Interview with Edward F. Edinger." In *Journal of Jungian Theory and Practice,* vol. 1 (Fall 1999).

Jerome Biblical Commentary. Ed. R.E. Brown, J.A. Fitzmyer, R.E. Murphy. London: Geoffrey Chapman, 1968.

Johnson, Robert. *The Fisher King and the Handless Maiden.* New York: HarperCollins, 1995.

_____. *We: Understanding the Psychology of Romantic Love.* New York: HarperCollins, 1983.

Jung, C.G. *C.G. Jung Letters* (Bollingen Series XCV). 2 vols. Ed. Gerhard Adler and Aniela Jaffé. Princeton: Princeton University Press, 1973.

_____. *The Collected Works*. (Bollingen Series XX) 20 vols. Trans. R.F.C. Hull. Ed. H. Read, M. Fordham, G. Adler, Wm. McGuire. Princeton: Princeton University Press, 1953-1979.

_____. *Memories, Dreams, Reflections*. Ed. Aniela Jaffé. Trans. Richard and Clara Winston. New York: Random House, 1965.

_____. *The Undiscovered Self*. Trans. R.F.C. Hull. New York: Mentor Book, New American Library, 1958.

_____. *The Visions Seminars, 1930-1934*. 2 vols. Zurich: Spring, 1976.

Jung, Emma, and von Franz, Marie-Louise. *The Grail Legend*. Trans. Andrea Dykes. Princeton: Princeton University Press, 1998.

Kosinski, Jerzy. *Being There*. New York: Bantam Books, 1972.

Larsen, Stephen, and Larsen, Robin. *A Fire in the Mind: The Life of Joseph Campbell*. New York: Anchor Books, Doubleday, 1991.

Lawrence, D.H. *Apocalypse*. London: Penguin Books, 1995.

_____. *Lady Chatterley's Lover*. London: Penguin Books, 1944.

Lehane, Brendan. *The Power of Plants*. New York: McGraw-Hill, 1977.

Meier, C.A. *Healing Dream and Ritual: Ancient Incubation and Modern Psychotherapy*. Einsiedeln, Switzerland: Daimon Verlag, 1989.

Messervy, Julie Moir. *The Inward Garden: Creating a Place of Beauty and Meaning*. New York: Little Brown and Company, 1995.

Moore, Hastings, and Moore, Gary W., eds. *The Neighbourhood of IS: Approaches to the Inner Solitude* (A Thematic Anthology). Lanham, MD: University Press of America, 1984.

Mulas, Antonia, photographer. *Eros in Antiquity*. New York: Erotic Art Book Society, 1978.

Norton Anthology of Poetry. 3rd edition. Ed. Alexander Alison et al. New York: W.W. Norton and Company, 1983.

O'Kane, F. *Sacred Chaos: Reflections on God's Shadow and the Dark Self*. Toronto: Inner City Books, 1994.

Otto, Rudolf. *The Idea of the Holy*. Trans. John W. Harvey. London: Oxford

University Press, 1958.

Pasternak, Boris. *Doctor Zhivago*. Trans. M. Hayward and M. Harari. New York: Pantheon Books, 1958.

Roche, Paul. " 'Eye for Eye, Tooth for Tooth': War, Reciprocity and Solidarity in Papua New Guinea. Some Lessons for the Modern World?" Lecture Series. Toronto: University of St. Michael's College, 1995-96.

Sawyer, Ruth. *The Way of the Storyteller*. New York: Penguin, 1990.

Sharp, Daryl. *Jung Lexicon: A Primer of Terms and Concepts*. Toronto: Inner City Books, 1991.

Solzhenitsyn, Alexander. *Cancer Ward*. Trans. N. Bethel and D. Burg. New York: Bantam Books, 1981.

Steinsaltz, Adin. *The Thirteen-Petalled Rose*. Trans. Y. Hanegbi. New York: Basic Books, 1980.

St. Ignatius. *The Spiritual Exercises*. Trans. Anthony Mottola. Garden City, NY: Doubleday, 1964.

Turner, Victor. "Betwixt and Between: Liminal Periods in Rites of Passage." In *Betwixt and Between: Patterns of Masculine and Feminine Initiation*. Eds. L.C. Mahdi, S. Foster, M. Little. LaSalle, IL: Open Court, 1988.

van Gennepp, Arnold. *The Rites of Passage*. Chicago: University of Chicago Press, 1960.

von Franz, Marie-Louise. *Alchemical Active Imagination*. Boston: Shambala, 1997.

_____. *Archetypal Patterns in Fairy Tales*. Toronto: Inner City Books, 1997.

_____. *The Golden Ass of Apuleius: The Liberation of the Feminine in Men*. Boston: Shambala, 1992.

_____. *Individuation in Fairy Tales*. Zurich: Spring Publications, 1977.

_____. *On Dreams and Death: A Jungian Interpretation*. Trans. E. Kennedy-Xipolitas and Vernon Brooks. Chicago, IL: Open Court, 1998.

_____. *Psychotherapy*. Boston: Shambala, 1993.

Wilhelm, Richard. *The Secret of the Golden Flower: A Chinese Book of Life*. London: Routledge & Kegan Paul, 1987.

Woolf, Virginia. *A Room of One's Own*. London: Grafton Books, 1977.

Index

Entries in *italics* refer to illustrations

Studies in Jungian Psychology
by Jungian Analysts

Quality Paperbacks

Prices and payment in $US (except in Canada, $Cdn)

Creating a Life: Finding Your Individual Path
James Hollis (Houston) ISBN 0-919123-93-7. 160 pp. $18

Jung and Yoga: The Psyche-Body Connection
Judith Harris (London, Ontario) ISBN 0-919123-95-3. 160 pp. $18

Jungian Psychology Unplugged: My Life as an Elephant
Daryl Sharp (Toronto) ISBN 0-919123-81-3. 160 pp. $18

Conscious Femininity: Interviews with Marion Woodman
Introduction by Marion Woodman (Toronto) ISBN 0-919123-59-7. 160 pp. $18

The Middle Passage: From Misery to Meaning in Midlife
James Hollis (Houston) ISBN 0-919123-60-0. 128 pp. $16

Eros and Pathos: Shades of Love and Suffering
Aldo Carotenuto (Rome) ISBN 0-919123-39-2. 144 pp. $18

Descent to the Goddess: A Way of Initiation for Women
Sylvia Brinton Perera (New York) ISBN 0-919123-05-8. 112 pp. $16

Addiction to Perfection: The Still Unravished Bride
Marion Woodman (Toronto) ISBN 0-919123-11-2. Illustrated. 208 pp. $20

The Illness That We Are: A Jungian Critique of Christianity
John P. Dourley (Ottawa) ISBN 0-919123-16-3. 128 pp. $16

Coming To Age: The Croning Years and Late-Life Transformation
Jane R. Prétat (Providence) ISBN 0-919123-63-5. 144 pp. $18

Jungian Dream Interpretation: A Handbook of Theory and Practice
James A. Hall, M.D. (Dallas) ISBN 0-919123-12-0. 128 pp. $16

Phallos: Sacred Image of the Masculine
Eugene Monick (Scranton) ISBN 0-919123-26-0. 30 illustrations. 144 pp. $18

The Sacred Prostitute: Eternal Aspect of the Feminine
Nancy Qualls-Corbett (Birmingham) ISBN 0-919123-31-7. 20 illustrations. 176 pp. $20

Personality Types: Jung's Model of Typology
Daryl Sharp (Toronto) ISBN 0-919123-30-9. 128 pp. $16

The Eden Project: In Search of the Magical Other
James Hollis (Houston) ISBN 0-919123-80-5. 160 pp. $18

Discounts: any 3-5 books, 10%; 6-9 books, 20%; 10 or more, 25%

Add Postage/Handling: 1-2 books, $6 surface ($10 air); 3-4 books, $8 surface ($12 air); 5-9 books, $15 surface ($20 air); 10 books or more, $10 surface ($25 air)

Ask for **Jung at Heart** newsletter and free Catalogue of **over 100 titles**

INNER CITY BOOKS

Box 1271, Station Q, Toronto, ON M4T 2P4, Canada

Tel. (416) 927-0355 / Fax (416) 924-1814 / E-mail: sales@innercitybooks.net